IELTS 考试技能训练教程

Writing Strategies for the IELTS Test

写 作

王 玉 西 编著

北京语言文化大学出国人员培训部

北京语言文化大学出版社

（京）新登字 157 号

图书在版编目（CIP）数据

IELTS考试技能训练教程：写作/王玉西编著．－北京：北京语言文化大学出版社，
1998（重印）
ISBN 7－5619－0543－2

Ⅰ．Ⅰ…

Ⅱ．王…

Ⅲ．①英语－高等学校－入学考试－英国－自学参考资料
②英语－写作－高等学校－入学考试－英国－自学参考资料

Ⅳ．H31

责任印制：孙　健
出版发行：北京语言文化大学出版社
　　　　　（北京海淀区学院路 15 号　邮政编码 100083）
印　　刷：北京林业大学印刷厂
经　　销：全国新华书店
版　　次：1997 年 3 月第 1 版　1998 年 4 月第 2 次印刷
开　　本：787×1092 毫米　1/16　印张：16
字　　数：250 千字　印数：3001－6000 册
定　　价：24.00 元

前　　言

　　《IELTS 考试技能训练教程》（以下简称《教程》）是北京语言文化大学出国人员培训部数名教员以七年多的对 IELTS 考生进行应考培训的经验为基础、对 IELTS 考试进行细致分析之后编写而成的。《教程》共分四册：

　　《听力》
　　《口语》
　　《阅读》
　　《写作》

　　《教程》具有以下特点：

　　1. 针对性强：《教程》针对 IELTS 考试而编写，读者对象为准备参加 IELTS 考试的人。通过做练习可使读者熟悉 IELTS 试题的模式，同时发现自己的弱点，做到知己知彼。

　　2. 练习形式多样化：IELTS 考试与其他几种英语考试（如 TOEFL、EPT）相比，具有题型更加多样化的特点。这些题型并不统一地存在于各次 IELTS 考试中。因此，熟悉各种题型是在考试中取得理想分数的一个关键。《教程》为读者提供了有针对性的、系统的训练，可使读者在考试中更好地发挥自己的能力。

　　3. 练习经过多年试用：《教程》中所有练习均在北京语言文化大学出国人员培训部经过使用和改进，在教学中收到良好的效果，受到学生的普遍欢迎，并得到英、美专家的指正，是作者多年辛勤工作的结晶。

　　4. 练习题材广泛：《教程》练习内容涉及生活中的许多方面以及自然科学和社会科学的多个领域，适用于从事各类工作的人。

　　5. 亦适用于参加其他考试的人：近年来语言教学理论强调语言能力而不是语言知识，强调语言的使用而不是用法。这些理论对语言测试亦有颇大影响。《教程》遵循 IELTS 考试的指导思想，注重培养学生使用英语，特别是以英语为工具从事专业学习和研究的能力。这种能力对参加任何英语考试都至关重要。

　　《教程》经过七年的孕育终于和读者见面，了却作者的一桩心事。但因恐"误人子弟"之怨，心情并未由此而轻松许多，因为书中难免有失误和不妥之处。欢迎读者提出意见。

《IELTS 考试技能训练教程·写作》简介

IELTS 考试是由英国文化委员会、剑桥大学地方考试委员会和澳大利亚大学联合会国际发展项目共同主办的一项考试。目的在于以此为标准招收留学生。此考试自 1980 年开办以来已发展到在一百多个国家和地区设有考点。据统计，1987 年的考生人数为一万四千多人。中国引进此项考试是在 80 年代末期。考点设在北京、上海、成都。

参加 IELTS 考试的人员都具备一定的英语基础，但考试结果却往往不能令人满意，其中一个突出的问题是由于他们的写作成绩不高，因而影响了考试的总成绩。这主要是因为他们写作基本功不够扎实，对于 IELTS 写作测试的特点、形式及写作技巧缺乏系统的认识。《IELTS 考试技能训练教程·写作》就是为了让考生充分了解 IELTS 写作测试、提高写作水平而编写的一本教科书。

本书共分五部分。第一部分和第五部分共有八套模拟写作试题。设置这两部分的目的是使考生了解试题的形式及大概内容，同时也使考生在开始使用这本教材时进行一次自我水平测试，明确自己的问题和差距，以便在后来的学习中加以弥补或改正；在结束使用这本教材时检查一下自己的进步幅度。

第二部分是语言诊断测试题，由拼写、语法、句型结构三套语言诊断测试题组成。设置此部分的目的是使考生通过拼写、语法和句型结构练习提高基础语言写作水平，以便达到或接近 IELTS 所需要的水平。这部分也可称为语言准备或调理阶段。

第三部分是常用写作手法。重点讲授 IELTS 考试中常出现的七种写作手法：记叙文、比较与对比、原因与结果、描述、议论文、报告、信件写作。

第四部分是测试技巧。共分六讲：审题、写提纲、写导语、写正文、写结尾、检查写作。

第五部分之后是部分练习答案及范文。在附录中，提供了 IELTS 考试简介和写作测试评分标准。

本教材适用于具有中等英语水平的出国留学生、研究生、大专院校学生、各种类型的英语培训班成年学员及自学者。

下面介绍教材的使用方法：

1. 教材使用者应选做第一部分中的一套或几套试题，对照范文检查自己的作文中所出现的问题或按照写作测试评分标准判定一下自己的分数。

2. 按要求做第二部分的练习，然后对照答案找问题，并加以解决。

3. 第三部分和第四部分是本教材的重点。为了加深对每课内容的理解，可采用先做练习，然后再讲解的方法；为了保证写作练习的效果，也可采用先看讲解然后再做练习的方法。

4. 由于各课内容有所不同，教材也采用了不同的练习形式。使用者在做完练习后可自对答案或参考范文，也可采用教师课堂讲评或学生互相讨论的方法。

　　5．第一部分和第五部分可用来进行模拟测试训练。如果有条件，应采用集体写作测试的形式，给学生创造一个测试环境，使他们积累一些测试经验。

　　由于作者水平有限，教材中缺点和疏漏在所难免。敬请读者指正。

作者　1996 年
于北京语言文化大学

Contents （目录）

Part One: Sample Tests

（第一部分：模拟试题）

1. Sample Test One
（模拟试题一）

WRITING TASK 1

You should spend about 20 minutes on this task.

Task:

*As a class assignment you have been asked to describe
an automatic electric oven.*

Describe an automatic electric oven, and explain how it works.

You may use your own knowledge and experience in addition to the diagram.

Your description should be:
1. relevant to the task, and
2. well organized.

You should write at least 150 words.

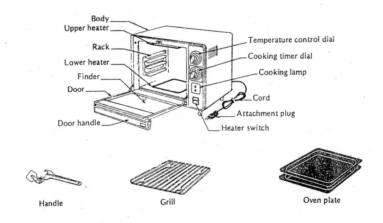

WRITING TASK 2

You should spend about 40 minutes on this task.

Task:

Write an essay for a university teacher on the following topic:

How much risk is acceptable in the pursuit of scientific and technological progress?

Give reasons for your answer.

You should write at least 250 words.

You should use your own ideas, knowledge and experience and support your arguments with examples and relevant evidence.

In writing your essay, you should remember that:
1. the essay must be well organized
2. your point of view must be clearly expressed, and
3. your argument must be supported by relevant evidence.

2. Sample Test Two
（模拟试题二）

WRITING TASK 1

You should spend about 20 minutes on this task.

Task:

> As a class assignment your tutor has asked you to write about a heart-lung machine. Using the diagram below, write three or four paragraphs describing the circulation of the blood on by-pass through a heart-lung machine.

You may use your own knowledge and experience in addition to the diagram.

Your description should be:
1. relevant to the task, and
2. well organized.

You should write at least 150 words.

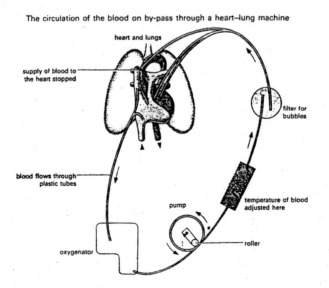

The circulation of the blood on by-pass through a heart—lung machine

heart and lungs

supply of blood to
the heart stopped

filter for
bubbles

blood flows through
plastic tubes

pump

temperature of blood
adjusted here

roller

oxygenator

WRITING TASK 2

You should spend about 40 minutes on this task.

Task:

Write an essay for a university teacher on the following topic:

"Education about diet is the most essential feature of a country's health-care programme." Is this a justified assumption?

Give your reasons for your answer.

You should write at least 250 words.

You should use your own ideas, knowledge and experience and support your arguments with examples and relevant evidence.

In writing your essay, you should remember that:
  1. the essay must be well organized
  2. your point of view must be clearly expressed, and
  3. your argument must be supported by relevant evidence.

3. Sample Test Three
(模拟试题三)

WRITING TASK 1

You should spend about 20 minutes on this task.

Task:

The diagram below illustrates a patterned plan of essay writing. Write three or four paragraphs to describe the plan and consider whether any changes are necessary.

You may use your own knowledge and experience in addition to the diagram.

Your description should be:
  1. relevant to the task, and
  2. well organized.

You should write at least 150 words.

A Patterned Plan of Essay Writing
Analyzing the Task
↓
Preparing a Plan
↓
Collecting Relevant Information
↓
Writing up
↓
Checking Your Writing

WRITING TASK 2

You should spend about 40 minutes on this task.

Task:

> As a class assignment you have been asked to write an essay on the following topic:
>
> Discuss the question of the death penalty in general. How far do you think it is justified?
>
> Give reasons for your answer.

Your should write at least 250 words.

You should use your own ideas, knowledge and experience and support your arguments with examples and relevant evidence.

In writing your essay, you should remember that:
1. the essay must be well organized
2. your point of view must be clearly expressed, and
3. your argument must be supported by relevant evidence.

4. Sample Test Four
（模拟试题四）

WRITING TASK 1

You should spend about 20 minutes on this task.

You want to rent a flat in Edinburgh University. You want to know something suitable for someone of your age and in your situation.

Task:

Write a letter to the Student Accommodation Office in the University telling them what your situation is, what accommodation you wish to have and ask for any suggestions.

You should write at least 150 words.

You do NOT need to write your address.

Begin your letter as follows:

Student Accommodation Office
30 Buccleuch Place,
Edinburgh EH8 9JS

Dear ...,

WRITING TASK 2

You should spend about 40 minutes on this task.

You are completing an application to a British university for an overseas scholarship. At the end of the application form you are asked to write a report in support of your application. It will not take the form of a letter.

Task:

Write briefly what you have already done in your own field, and what you wish to do in the future course.

You should write at least 250 words.

Part Two: Diagnostic Tests [ˌdaiəgˈnɔstik]

（第二部分：诊断测试）

1．Test One：Spelling
（测试一：拼写）

1.1. The following are 100 incorrectly spelt words. Correct each of them and then copy the right one on the line beside.

1. bandoned ＿＿＿＿＿＿ 2. childrern ＿＿＿＿＿＿

3. stoped ＿＿＿＿＿＿ 4. abruply ＿＿＿＿＿＿

5. sousand ＿＿＿＿＿＿ 6. acelerate ＿＿＿＿＿＿

7. recuvery ＿＿＿＿＿＿ 8. allmost ＿＿＿＿＿＿

9. allert ＿＿＿＿＿＿ 10. ambigous ＿＿＿＿＿＿

11. imposible ＿＿＿＿＿＿ 12. asignment ＿＿＿＿＿＿

13. asume ＿＿＿＿＿＿ 14. arived ＿＿＿＿＿＿

15. behaivior ＿＿＿＿＿＿ 16. becouse ＿＿＿＿＿＿

17. canciled ＿＿＿＿＿＿ 18. colleage ＿＿＿＿＿＿

19. recives ＿＿＿＿＿＿ 20. conffident ＿＿＿＿＿＿

21. suparvisor ＿＿＿＿＿＿ 22. lecturar ＿＿＿＿＿＿

23. governement ＿＿＿＿＿＿ 24. sektion ＿＿＿＿＿＿

25. examenation ＿＿＿＿＿＿ 26. proposel ＿＿＿＿＿＿

27. contrery ＿＿＿＿＿＿ 28. oposite ＿＿＿＿＿＿

29. sistem ＿＿＿＿＿＿ 30. inferr ＿＿＿＿＿＿

31. analisys ＿＿＿＿＿＿ 32. develepment ＿＿＿＿＿＿

33. fasilities ＿＿＿＿＿＿ 34. apropriate ＿＿＿＿＿＿

35. knowlege ＿＿＿＿＿＿ 36. excede ＿＿＿＿＿＿

37. fraimwork ＿＿＿＿＿＿ 38. progres ＿＿＿＿＿＿

39. cronological ＿＿＿＿＿＿ 40. responsability ＿＿＿＿＿＿

41. resourse ＿＿＿＿＿＿ 42. experriment ＿＿＿＿＿＿

43. charactarise ＿＿＿＿＿＿ 44. gradualy ＿＿＿＿＿＿

45. laborotory ＿＿＿＿＿＿ 46. paralel ＿＿＿＿＿＿

47. psichological ＿＿＿＿＿＿ 48. concreet ＿＿＿＿＿＿

49. crytisism ＿＿＿＿＿＿ 50. persuit ＿＿＿＿＿＿

51. questionnare ＿＿＿＿＿＿ 52. moddification ＿＿＿＿＿＿

53. distrebution ＿＿＿＿＿＿ 54. discribe ＿＿＿＿＿＿

55. assinement ＿＿＿＿＿＿ 56. comparitive ＿＿＿＿＿＿

57. significent ＿＿＿＿＿＿ 58. sustanable ＿＿＿＿＿＿

59. eqipment ＿＿＿＿＿＿ 60. approches ＿＿＿＿＿＿

61. weaknes	_____	62. apparartus	_____
63. approximatly	_____	64. measurment	_____
65. decreese	_____	66. seaqential	_____
67. obsurve	_____	68. attemt	_____
69. perspectife	_____	70. multipel	_____
71. elementery	_____	72. simultanous	_____
73. corelation	_____	74. discusion	_____
75. emfasise	_____	76. variabillity	_____
77. involvment	_____	78. beleif	_____
79. significanse	_____	80. recegnise	_____
81. sumarise	_____	82. sinthesise	_____
83. seperate	_____	84. estimete	_____
85. paramater	_____	86. polisy	_____
87. inevitablly	_____	88. predominently	_____
89. materiel	_____	90. efficency	_____
91. riview	_____	92. consumtion	_____
93. abundence	_____	94. seoretical	_____
95. graphik	_____	96. achievment	_____
97. recieve	_____	98. responce	_____
99. patern	_____	100. aquire	_____

1.2. The following list contains 120 words commonly found in academic writing. Fifty of these words are spelt incorrectly. Locate and correct the incorrectly spelt words.

1. congeston	_____	2. dilema	_____
3. theory	_____	4. thesis	_____
5. doutful	_____	6. tutor	_____
7. seminar	_____	8. durration	_____
9. examinaition	_____	10. vitamines	_____
11. emergy	_____	12. department	_____
13. justification	_____	14. esential	_____
15. eforts	_____	16. futil	_____
17. justify	_____	18. centery	_____
19. feature	_____	20. conclusion	_____
21. divided	_____	22. anually	_____
23. penertrated	_____	24. permernently	_____
25. objective	_____	26. hypothesis	_____
27. postboned	_____	28. rutine	_____

29. benefits _____
30. operate _____
31. position _____
32. accomodation _____
33. achive _____
34. surpass _____
35. fluctuation _____
36. crucial _____
37. aplicable _____
38. begining _____
39. collige _____
40. predict _____
41. outline _____
42. specific _____
43. corect _____
44. attitude _____
45. expirimental _____
46. investigation _____
47. hierarchy _____
48. increesingly _____
49. insuficient _____
50. knowlege _____
51. determine _____
52. implication _____
53. mantaining _____
54. necesary _____
55. opinion _____
56. effectiveness _____
57. comprehensive _____
58. contradiction _____
59. refering _____
60. reserch _____
61. especially _____
62. studing _____
63. teckniques _____
64. univercity _____
65. whitch _____
66. methodology _____
67. challenge _____
68. abstract _____
69. carier _____
70. critisism _____
71. appendices _____
72. performance _____
73. dissappeared _____
74. emphersis _____
75. conditions _____
76. details _____
77. structure _____
78. provide _____
79. conduct _____
80. forienger _____
81. findings _____
82. outcome _____
83. report _____
84. essay _____
85. differ _____
86. interwiewed _____
87. lovelly _____
88. relatively _____
89. systematically _____
90. medisine _____
91. standard _____
92. literature _____
93. ocupation _____
94. resourses _____
95. comparison _____
96. awareness _____
97. programming _____
98. yield _____
99. thurough _____
100. wheather _____
101. analytical _____
102. application _____
103. planning _____
104. further _____
105. strengths _____
106. writting _____

107. statistical	_____	108. activate	_____
109. conventional	_____	110. affect	_____
111. enable	_____	112. expect	_____
113. select	_____	114. exclude	_____
115. hieght	_____	116. establish	_____
117. factor	_____	118. institude	_____
119. influence	_____	120. succesful	_____

1.3. Translate the following English into Chinese:

1. stabilisation	_____	2. dramatically	_____
3. design	_____	4. continuous	_____
5. assessment	_____	6. orientation	_____
7. consider	_____	8. future	_____
9. emission	_____	10. allocation	_____
11. distribute	_____	12. limitation	_____
13. concentration	_____	14. adopt	_____
15. assume	_____	16. diverse	_____
17. vary	_____	18. lengthen	_____
19. specify	_____	20. produce	_____
21. author	_____	22. frequently	_____
23. configuration	_____	24. specification	_____
25. minor	_____	26. phase	_____
27. concern	_____	28. depletion	_____
29. simulator	_____	30. sample	_____
31. per capita	_____	32. relationship	_____
33. quantitative	_____	34. bibliography	_____
35. serve	_____	36. role	_____
37. consistency	_____	38. quote	_____
39. ensure	_____	40. edit	_____
41. employ	_____	42. redundant	_____
43. irrelevant	_____	44. depth	_____
45. match	_____	46. correspond	_____
47. common	_____	48. experience	_____
49. animal	_____	50. natural	_____
51. instinct	_____	52. rational	_____
53. prudence	_____	54. lame	_____
55. cowardice	_____	56. biological	_____
57. expediency	_____	58. sensibly	_____

59. moral _____
60. subject _____
61. anthropologist _____
62. unsatisfactory _____
63. particular _____
64. society _____
65. circumstance _____
66. consideration _____
67. primitive _____
68. contrast _____
69. aspect _____
70. action _____
71. ancient _____
72. athletic _____
73. religious _____
74. association _____
75. festival _____
76. honour _____
77. eventually _____
78. character _____
79. international _____
80. exactly _____
81. protest _____
82. suggestion _____
83. commercial _____
84. television _____
85. license _____
86. condition _____
87. devote _____
88. programme _____
89. definite _____
90. allow _____
91. assumption _____
92. justify _____
93. individual _____
94. compose _____
95. benefit _____
96. submit _____
97. compulsory _____
98. attendance _____
99. proper _____
100. commonly _____

1.4. Translate the following Chinese into English：

1. 传达;运送(动) _____
2. 降低;使萧条(动) _____
3. 出口;排水口(名) _____
4. 输出量;产量(名) _____
5. 景色;观点(名) _____
6. 避免(动) _____
7. 让步(动) _____
8. 包括(动) _____
9. 分裂(动) _____
10. 已废弃的(形) _____
11. 连续的(形) _____
12. 严重的(形) _____
13. 外部的(形) _____
14. 内部的(形) _____
15. (时间的)间隔(名) _____
16. 提高;增进(动) _____
17. 从事;承担(动) _____
18. 遭受;忍受(动) _____
19. 加重(动) _____
20. 侵略(名) _____
21. 自由(名) _____
22. 设备(名) _____
23. 调查(名) _____
24. 节日(名) _____
25. 成熟的(形) _____
26. 点(名) _____
27. 使颠倒(动) _____
28. 同一的(形) _____
29. 有罪的(形) _____
30. 无罪的(形) _____

31. 消失(动) _____
32. 不赞成(动) _____
33. 举止;行为(名) _____
34. 例行公事(名) _____
35. 效率(名) _____
36. 准确;精确(名) _____
37. 准确的(形) _____
38. 完成(动) _____
39. 有效的(形) _____
40. 重点(名) _____
41. 自信的(形) _____
42. 适当的;足够的(形) _____
43. 延期(动) _____
44. 前面的(形) _____
45. 后面的(形) _____
46. 兴趣(名) _____
47. 犹豫(名) _____
48. 分离(动) _____
49. 顶点(名) _____
50. 因而;所以(副) _____
51. 准确地(副) _____
52. 然而;不过(连) _____
53. 比率(名) _____
54. 种类(名) _____
55. 具体的(形) _____
56. 一般的(形) _____
57. 最大量(名) _____
58. 最大的(形) _____
59. 最小量(名) _____
60. 最小的(形) _____
61. 近似的(形) _____
62. 可靠的(形) _____
63. 干涉(动) _____
64. 混乱(名) _____
65. 混乱的(形) _____
66. 天然的;粗糙的(形) _____
67. 本来地;最初地(副) _____
68. 蒸发(动) _____
69. 由……组成(动) _____
70. 连接(名) _____
71. 加强(动) _____
72. 会员;资格(名) _____
73. 可靠性(名) _____
74. 不可避免的(形) _____
75. 限制(动) _____
76. 索引(名) _____
77. 指导教师(名) _____
78. 被禁止的(形) _____
79. 偶然的行动(名) _____
80. 显而易见的(形) _____
81. 明显的(形) _____
82. 值得考虑的(形) _____
83. 推荐(动) _____
84. 满期(动) _____
85. 交换(动) _____
86. 居民(名) _____
87. 刺激;激发(动) _____
88. 广泛的(形) _____
89. 象征(名) _____
90. 不可抵抗的(形) _____
91. 强制的;义务的(形) _____
92. 自愿的(形) _____
93. 卷;册(名) _____
94. 外行人(名) _____
95. 不寻常(形) _____
96. 中立的;中性的(形) _____
97. 原则(名) _____
98. 改革(名) _____
99. 证实(动) _____
100. 吸收(动) _____

2. Test Two: Grammar
（测试二：语法）

There are 100 items in this section. There are four words or phrases, marked a, b, c, d beneath each sentence. Choose the one word or phrase that best completes the sentence. Mark your answer by blackening the corresponding letter.

1. The public . . . interested in talking about the news.
   a. has been   b. are   c. was   d. is

2. . . . were looking forward to working overtime.
   a. None office workers   b. None of the office worker
   c. None of the office workers   d. None of office worker

3. Do adjectives come before nouns or after them in . . . ?
   a. the French language   b. a French language
   c. French language   d. language of French

4. A compound consists of atoms . . . different chemical properties.
   a. of   b. by
   c. for   d. with

5. I apologise . . . her . . . my impoliteness.
   a. with; to   b. to; for
   c. for; to   d. on; for

6. He changed his car . . . a foreign make.
   a. for   b. to
   c. from   d. with

7. He had lived in Paris for some years . . . he returned to America.
   a. after   b. until
   c. before   d. while

8. John is the cleverest of . . . in Class Two.
   a. any other student   b. any of the students
   c. anyone of the students   d. all the students

9. The moment I . . . my drawing, we . . . to the playground for physical training.
   a. finish; go   b. have finished; will go
   c. shall finish; will be going   d. would finish; shall go

10. No one will go out in the downpour, . . . ?

18

a. will he   b. won't he
c. will they   d. won't they

11. Never before in China ... for the farmers.
    a. has so much been done   b. have so much been done
    c. has been done so much   d. so much has been done

12. Mary came to see the mountain and ... .
    a. stayed enjoying it   b. stayed to enjoying
    c. stayed to enjoy   d. stayed to enjoy it

13. It was so ... done that John felt like applauding.
    a. beautiful   b. beautifully
    c. good   d. fine

14. Because the rooms ... , we have not moved in yet.
    a. are being painted   b. were painted
    c. have been painted   d. having painted

15. These compounds could not have been formed if the chemical reaction ...
    stopped.
    a. have been   b. has been
    c. had been   d. were

16. The house is found ... down.
    a. to burn   b. burning
    c. having burned   d. to have been burned

17. Comrade Li was found ... at great attention in the library.
    a. being worked   b. working
    c. work   d. having worked

18. ... was the correct distance from the earth to the moon.
    a. Newton did not know at first what
    b. Newton did not know what at first
    c. What Newton did not know at first
    d. What did Newton not know at first

19. Don't let me disturb you; please get ... your typing.
    a. with   b. in with
    c. on with   d. in

20. We ... always keep these words in mind. They ... give us courage and
    strength.
    a. have to; need to   b. would; should
    c. should; will   d. must; dare to

21. Sixty percent of the liquid ... alcohol.
    a. have to be   b. are
    c. were to be   d. is

19

22. Wang Li is one of the brightest students who ... from Beijing University.
    a. is graduated
    b. have graduated
    c. has graduated
    d. had graduated
23. He has just been appointed ... member of the club.
    a. a honorary
    b. the honorary
    c. an honorary
    d. honorary
24. Hot air accompanied by high relative humidity feels warmer than.... .
    a. is it actually
    b. it actually is
    c. actually it is
    d. is actually it
25. Don't walk ... the street ... traffic light turns green.
    a. across; to
    b. on; until
    c. in; until
    d. across; until
26. Did you burn a big hole in the carpet ... a cigarette?
    a. from
    b. on
    c. by
    d. with
27. Please look through these papers ... your leisure.
    a. on
    b. in
    c. for
    d. at
28. Let us go near a fire ... we may get warm.
    a. when
    b. so that
    c. before
    d. such that
29. There is no greater happiness ... who wins honour for his country.
    a. than a man
    b. than a man's
    c. than that of a man
    d. than that of a man's
30. At this time on Monday I ... the calculation for the last time.
    a. shall be doing
    b. shall do
    c. shall have done
    d. do
31. They ... swimming, but now they ... used to it.
    a. don't like; have been
    b. didn't like; are
    c. have not liked; are being
    d. didn't like; will be
32. I haven't seen Lao Li these past few days. I'm afraid   he ... himself for some time.
    a. wasn't feeling
    b. isn't feeling
    c. hadn't been feeling
    d. hasn't been feeling
33. I only speak English ... a little Spanish.
    a. nor
    b. so
    c. but
    d. and
34. ... he would not have failed the final exam.

a. Xiao Chang were a little more hardworking,

b. Should Xiao Chang be a little more hardworking,

c. If Xiao Chang were a little more hardworking,

d. Had Xiao Chang been a little more hardworking,

35. Only in the last few days ... to repair the swimming pool.

    a. anything has been done   b. has done anything

    c. has anything been done   d. has there anything been done

36. I saw her water-skiing on the lake and, finally, ... into it.

    a. fell   b. falling

    c. being fallen   d. to fall

37. Until yesterday, his family ... from him for six months.

    a. hasn't heard   b. hadn't heard

    c. hasn't been hearing   d. hadn't hearing

38. The wounded ... to the hospitals down the village.

    a. has been carried   b. had carried

    c. were carried   d. was being carried

39. He looks sleepy. He must ... to bed very late last night.

    a. had gone   b. have gone

    c. be going   d. go

40. She didn't like herself ... like that.

    a. praising   b. to be praised

    c. having praised   d. that she had been praised

41. We watched ... football.

    a. that John play   b. John play

    c. John to play   d. John for playing

42. I wonder ... in such a heavy rain.

    a. he has got back what   b. which he has got back

    c. how he has got back   d. how has he got back

43. The theory ... is easy for us to understand.

    a. liquids that tend to expand when heated

    b. that liquids tend to expand when heated

    c. that tend to expand liquids when heated

    d. when heated that liquids tend to expand

44. It is no use ... to get to the airport in half an hour.

    a. trying   b. having tried

    c. having been tried   d. being tried

45. ... fire, break the glass and sound the alarm.

    a. In case   b. In case of

    c. Owing to   d. Despite

46. The students must finish the test in . . .
    a. three quarters of an hour time.
    b. three quarter's of an hour time.
    c. three quarters of an hour 's time.
    d. three quarters' of an hour's time.

47. He can't bear . . . at night.
    a. having to work   b. have to work
    c. to have worked   d. to having worked

48. Either the postman or the driver must have eaten . . . lunch here.
    a. its   b. their
    c. theirs   d. his

49. Rosemary likes Lantao Island, and so . . . .
    a. her husband does   b. does her husband
    c. her husband is   d. is her husband

50. I want to borrow some books about history if you have . . . .
    a. a few   b. any
    c. many   d. much

51. She hopes that he . . . and see her again.
    a. shall come   b. will come
    c. come   d. comes

52. You'd like to spend your vacation in the States, . . . ?
    a. hadn't you   b. should you
    c. shouldn't you   d. wouldn't you

53. They arrived at 3 p.m. but the class . . . long before that.
    a. started   b. was starting
    c. had been starting   d. had started

54. They never dared to live in the haunted house, . . . ?
    a. dared they   b. daren't they
    c. weren't they   d. did they

55. . . . when he was knocked down by a heavy duty lorry.
    a. Hardly had he got to the pavement
    b. Hardly he had got to the pavement
    c. He got hardly to the pavement
    d. Hardly he got to the pavement

56. Her blouse didn't fit her well. . . .
    a. So her skirt didn't.   b. So didn't her skirt.
    c. But her skirt didn't.   d. But her skirt did.

57. There will be . . . of water unless it rains soon.
    a. shortage   b. the shortage

c. shortages   d. a shortage

58. Light travels ... the speed of 186,300 miles per second.

     a. in   b. by

     c. at   d. for

59. ... on that table belongs to me.

     a. The luggage   b. The luggages

     c. A luggage   d. Some luggages

60. Last Sunday an old man ... the street when he suddenly ... down.

     a. crossed; was falling   b. had crossed; had fallen

     c. was crossing; had fallen   d. was crossing; fell

61. Their ... of affectation, of hypocrisy.

     a. conducts savour   b. conduct savour

     c. conduct savours   d. conducts savours

62. After ten years, all those youngsters became ... .

     a. growns-ups   b. growns-up

     c. grown-up   d. grown-ups

63. The committee ... been arguing about the economic problems among themselves for many hours.

     a. have   b. has

     c. could have   d. can have

64. My English vocabulary ... quite limited.

     a. is   b. are

     c. have become   d. to be

65. A great deal of ... was done to crops.

     a. damages   b. damaging

     c. damage   d. ruin

66. He bought ... for his father in a drugstore.

     a. some medicine   b. some medicines

     c. many medicine   d. enough medicines

67. ... is covered with heavy snow.

     a. The earth's surface   b. The surface of earth

     c. The surface earth   d. The earth surface

68. In some restaurants, food and service are worse than ... used to be.

     a. they   b. it

     c. them   d. that

69. Every student should be encouraged to know... own potentialities.

     a. his   b. their

     c. one's   d. her

70. Even though computers operate without human prejudice, some people

fear that ... can be harmful to man.

    a. its logical solutions   b. logical solutions its'

    c. their logical solutions   d. them logical solutions

71. Existing reserves of fossil fuel ... by 2045.

    a. have been run out   b. will have run out

    c. is going to be run out   d. have run out

72. Only by investing heavily in value-added exports ... from the present trade imbalance.

    a. the country can emerge   b. the country might emerge

    c. can the country emerge   d. the country emerged

73. Until the 16th century the earth ... to be flat.

    a. is believed   b. has been believed

    c. believed   d. was believed

74. The more acid you add to the solution, ... it becomes.

    a. cloudier   b. the cloudier

    c. the cloudiest   d. more cloudy

75. After studying our experimental results, the tutor suggested that ... .

    a. us to repeat   b. that we to repeat

    c. we repeat   d. we to repeat

76. Only a few realized the damage they had caused. ... did run away in fright.

    a. The ones who   b. The ones whom

    c. Few who   d. Whom that

77. The boys in this street like to bully ... .

    a. each other   b. one and other

    c. one another   d. one and the other

78. The car I am driving is different from ... .

    a. that   b. that one

    c. that ones   d. those

79. One common family name is Wang; ... is Li.

    a. another   b. the other

    c. others   d. none other

80. I have two dictionaries: one is a Chinese-English dictionary, and ... is an English-Chinese one.

    a. another   b. the other

    c. other   d. none other

81. Some girls have one pig-tail; ... girls have two.

    a. another   b. the other

    c. other   d. one other

82. I don't like this wine. I like ... wine.
    a. some others   b. another
    c. other   d. some other
83. After ... your results you should make an appointment with your tutor.
    a. you receiving   b. you would have received
    c. you have received   d. you received
84. You ... the experiment twice, not once.
    a. should have carried out   b. shouldn't have carried out
    c. haven't carried out   d. couldn't have carried out
85. After receiving her results, the student stopped... .
    a. to worry   b. having worried
    c. worrying   d. to be worried
86. You ... include this section. It's not necessary.
    a. must   b. couldn't
    c. don't need   d. don't have to
87. Unless ... an extension at least one week before the due date, it will not
    be given.
    a. you request   b. you will request
    c. you requested   d. requesting
88. The scientists were prohibited ... the danger zone.
    a. to enter   b. entering
    c. enter   d. from entering
89. ... producing methane, the process also produces carbon monoxide.
    a. Apart   b. As well
    c. Besides   d. In addition
90. The biologist admitted ... excessive numbers of animals in laboratory
    tests.
    a. using   b. to use
    c. being used   d. used
91. He is ... that he often makes mistakes.
    a. a such careless man b. a so careless man
    c. such a careless man d. so a careless man
92. We can ... imagine what the world would be like without the sea.
    a. never hardly   b. not hardly
    c. no hardly   d. hardly
93. We have little ... farming.
    a. knowledge of or experience in
    b. knowledge in or experience with
    c. knowledge about or experience with

25

d. knowledge for or experience about

94. No sooner had he seen the blind man ... .
    a. than he got up from his chair
    b. when he got up from his chair
    c. so he got up from his chair
    d. therefore he got up from his chair

95. ... , but she wants to play it better.
    a. Mary is good at the violin
    b. Mary is a good violinist
    c. Although Mary plays the violin very well
    d. Mary plays the violin very well

96. The two rows of grinding machinery were placed so that there was plenty
    of walking space ... them.
    a. between   b. among
    c. along   d. for

97. By the end of the century, it is likely that the oceans of the world ... by
    all the rubbish poured into them.
    a. will be polluting   b. will have been polluted
    c. would have being polluted d. will pollute

98. I can speak German but ... you do.
    a. not as well as   b. not well than
    c. not so well than   d. not so better as

99. Please give me ... water. I'm thirsty.
    a. little   b. any more
    c. a few   d. a little

100. The test ... until all the classes are here.
    a. won't begin   b. will begin
    c. begins   d. is beginning

3. Test Three: Sentence Construction
(测试三：句型结构)

By using the words in brackets, join each of the following sentences into logical ones. You may need to change some of the words.

Example: He studies English. He studies French. (as well as)
        Sample answer: He studies English as well as French.

1. A student has studied English for a few years. He may have a vocabulary of thousands of words. (who)
2. Between formal and colloquial English there is unmarked English. It is neither so literary and serious as formal English, nor so casual and free as colloquial English. (which)
3. He bought a jeep. His friend advised him against it. (in spite of)
4. Good writing requires general and abstract words as well as specific and concrete ones. It is the latter that make writing vivid, real and clear. (though)
5. It was raining hard. They could not work in the fields. (so ... that)
6. The politician is concerned with successful elections. The statesman is interested in the future of his people. (whereas)
7. The results of the experiment were successful. The school refused to give any help. (although)
8. He chose to study computer science. Computer science has good employment prospects. (because of)
9. Mary walked very slowly. She did not catch the train. (if)
10. He is not coming. The meeting will be put off till next week. (in the event of)
11. I said yes yesterday. On second thoughts I must say no. (but)
12. A cautious driver always brings with him a spare tyre. He has a puncture. (in case)
13. Many people do not have enough to eat. There is plenty of food in the world. (however)
14. Nuclear power can be used to make electricity. Many people are against using nuclear power. (although)
15. All the oil in the world will soon be used up. We are not trying hard

enough to find new sources of energy. (but)

16. Without agriculture we could not feed ourselves. Agriculture is important to man. (because)

17. It would be rather impertinent of me to express an opinion. I am not a member of the Church of England myself. (therefore)

18. Computer chess games are still a bit expensive, but they are getting cheaper all the time. The chess-playing strength is rising. (furthermore)

19. The cream is separated from the milk. It is made into butter. (after)

20. The population of Nepal will double in the next 25 years. The population of some Asian countries is increasing rapidly. (for example)

21. Western Europe has large reserves of fuel. The UK has a 250 year supply of coal. (for instance)

22. A duck can swim easily and walk on soft ground. It has webbed feet. (so that)

23. Far fewer people are killed or injured during train travel. Rail travel is safer than road travel. (because)

24. An area of low pressure forms over the land. The heated air expands and rises. (as a result)

25. Canada is similar to the United States. The majority of its people speak English. (in that)

26. Governments will most probably not relocate entire cities. They are in earthquake zones. (just because)

27. They were forced to buy expensive ones. There were no economy seats available. (so)

28. The hypothesis could be tested. Two experiments were conducted. (so that)

29. Middle-class families tend to have person-centred structures. Working-class families are usually positional. (whereas)

30. Middle-class children do well in most education systems. Working-class children do relatively poorly. (on the other hand)

31. Lima, La Paz (Bolivia) and Lisbon are all capitals. Los Angeles is not. (however)

32. Mauritius, Iceland and Sri Lanka consist of one main island. New Zealand is formed by two. (while)

33. Whales, dolphins, kangaroos and man are warm-blooded. Snakes are not. (on the other hand)

34. The environmental component of intelligence differs from whatever is due to heredity. It is susceptible of manipulation. (in that)

35. The suffixes -er and -or mean "a person who". The suffixes -fy and -ize

signify "to make". (whereas)

36. The flight is an exhausting one. Most of the birds arrive safely. (however)

37. Hotels and food are cheap. The warm climate makes the country attractive for tourists. (in addition)

38. Eggs are cheap. Eggs are rich in protein. (moreover)

39. Smith accepts Brown's theory. He disagrees with some of his conclusions. (however)

40. Socioeconomic status has been shown to relate to attitudes to education. It is a predictor of academic attainment. (additionally)

41. Cows' principal source of food is grass. Lions are carnivores. (by way of contrast)

42. She liked the people. She could identify with them. (furthermore)

43. The government's education policy was occasionally problematic. The government's term of office was considered highly successful. (while)

44. The company's sales have declined in recent years. The company continues to hold a major share of the market. (despite the fact that)

45. There was a temporary recession in the early part of 1974. The decade was one of rapid economic growth. (in spite of the fact that)

46. The study has been widely acclaimed. A few criticisms have been made of the implications drawn by the researchers. (nevertheless)

47. The steel frames are covered with reinforced plastic film. It is resistant to weather. (that)

48. The plants are fed by inorganic nutrients dissolved in water. It is supplied by a plastic pipeline. (which)

49. The debris becomes ideal nuclei for the formation of ice crystals. It is exposed to iodine vapour. (when)

50. Letters and packets are taken to the sorting office. The bags are emptied and letters separated from the packets. (where)

Part Three：Common Writing Techniques in Testing

（第三部分：常用测试写作手法）

1. Narration 〔næ'rei∫ən〕

（记叙文） 叙述(法).故事

1.1. Narration, as a pattern of thought, consists of the act of following a sequence of actions or events in time. It is a recounting of the facts or particulars of some occurrence, incident, or experience.

The simplest kind of narration is the one which follows chronological order, i.e. which tells the events in the order in which they occurred.

Read the following paragraph:

> I went to the lecture at 11 o'clock. Before that I had a sandwich and a cup of coffee at the university canteen. I didn't have enough time to eat my breakfast. After the lecture, I went off and ate a big lunch.

Comment

This paragraph is not following the chronological order. It seems to be a bit jumbled. It is better to be written as follows:

> I got up late in the morning, so I didn't have enough time to eat my breakfast. Before I went to the lecture at 11 o'clock I had a sandwich and a cup of coffee at the university canteen. After the lecture, I went off and ate a big lunch.

Exercise 1

Read the sentences below. Then rearrange them in time order. Use the transition words and phrases and other clues to help you. Finally, rewrite the sentences as a narrative paragraph.

Group one:
  a. Braille decided to see if he could invent a system similar to night-writing to enable the blind to read.
  b. He met a captain Barbier who told him about a night-writing system

which soldiers could use to read in the dark.

   c. He did not think much of the methods of teaching the blind which were used at the special school.

   d. At the age of ten, he was sent to a special school for the blind.

   e. In his early twenties, he was successful and invented the Braille system, which is still in use today.

   f. Louis Braille was born in France in 1809.

   g. Braille was accidentally blinded when he was 3 years old.

Group Two:

   a. Aristide had gone for a walk in the forest one day.

   b. He set out early in the morning.

   c. He did not know how to find his way back to the town.

   d. He soon fell asleep.

   e. He was tired and hungry, and sat down to rest.

   f. Having walked for several hours, he suddenly realized that he was lost.

   g. He was surrounded by redskins.

   h. When he awoke, it was nearly dark.

   i. They bound his hands and led him away to their village.

Group Three:

   a. After a while, Tom neared home, dragging the sled.

   b. Smoke was coming from a side window near the stove.

   c. Even before he arrived, he could hear the sled dogs barking.

   d. Then he ripped flaming curtains from the wall.

   e. Immediately he rushed past the dogs and stormed into the cabin.

   f. Then as Tom came close to the cabin, he panicked.

   g. At last, he rushed out the front door with them, flinging them into the snow.

1.2. The Common Structure of Narration

The rhetorical structure of narration can be partially conveyed by a single sentence:

> Yesterday morning, on the main street in the city centre, Mr Wang had a car accident.

This sentence contains all the elements of narration (except cause and effect): the time (when the event occurred), the place (where the event occurred), the agent (the person or persons who take part in the action), and the action (the thing done).

Because narration follows the laws of chronological succession, in the narrative the pattern can be as follows:

Introduction (contains time, place, agent, and beginning of action)
Event 1
Event 2
Event 3

.

.

.

Conclusion

1.3. Narration often goes hand in hand with description. Practising writing a factual description of a place and a day's routine associated with the place is useful for an IELTS candidate. From this, he will learn to describe a workplace or educational institution and to describe the main facts of a person's working day in chronological order.

Read the following examples:

Example 1

A Senior Surgeon

Dr. Wang Ling works in Beijing No. 3 Hospital. The hospital is in the west of Beijing. It is one of a group of three hospitals.

About 360 people work in Beijing No. 3 Hospital. There are about 120 nurses, 90 doctors and 150 other hospital workers. Some of the doctors also work in other hospitals. The hospital has 12 wards and 250 beds for patients. Every day, there are four or five clinics for out-patients. The hospital is open twenty-four hours a day.

Wang Ling is a senior surgeon at the hospital. She arrives at work at about a quarter to eight. She operates every morning. She has lunch at about twelve o'clock. The break lasts about one hour. On Mondays and Thursdays, she has a clinic at two. She also visits her patients in the wards every day. She finishes work at around six. She goes to the hospital for emergencies at night and on Sundays.

Comment

The present simple tense in this narrative is used when writing about everyday routine. This is a very common use of this tense. The first paragraph is an introduction. The second one tells the person's workplace. The third is the day's work. This writing is very well organized.

Look at the following example:

Example 2

A Technician

Zhang Ming works on Platform No. 4 at the Stone oilfield. The Stone oilfield is in the South Sea. No. 4 is one of the ten oil production platforms at the oilfield. No. 4 is about 60 kilometres from the land.

Platform No. 4 stands in 90 metres of water and it is 25 metres high above the water. The platform area is 3,000 square metres. 120 people work on the platform.

Zhang Ming is a production technician. He operates and looks after the production machinery. He has breakfast at 7:00 a.m. and starts work at 8:00 a.m. At about twelve o'clock, he has a break for lunch. The break lasts for one hour. He finishes work at 8:00 p.m. After work, he has dinner and then watches television or plays games. He lives and works on the platform for one month. At the end of the month, he has a month's rest at home. Then he goes back to work for another month.

Exercise 2

Write about where you work or study, what time your day begins and finishes and what you do at work. Or write about another person's workplace and day's work.

The guide for the writing: (This guide may help you.)

(1) Introduction	—name of person
	—name of workplace
	—kind of place
	—where it is
(2) The workplace	—number of workers/students

—how big it is

—when it is open

—other interesting facts

(3) The day's work — kind of job

—when work starts

—times of breaks

—when work finishes

1.4. In real life, one is often required to write a personal factual narrative on particular events. It is therefore useful for the students to learn how to arrange the events in chronological order and to describe the events in a simple piece of continuous writing.

Read and study the following examples:

Example 1

A Picnic beside the Yellow River

Some years ago, I lived in Tengkou. I was a teacher in a secondary school. Every year, we had a class picnic. One year, we had a very enjoyable picnic beside the Yellow River.

We met at the school very early in the morning. One of the boys brought a chicken with him. We rode our bicycles beside the river for about six kilometres. We found a beautiful place under some trees.

All the students did different jobs. Some boys lit a fire and some girls brought water from the river. Two boys killed the chicken and prepared it for cooking. Some other girls prepared salad and cooked lots of rice. Everything was ready at 11 o'clock. And by that time we were all very hungry.

After the meal, we played volleyball. Later, the boys played football and the girls went swimming in the river. We drank a bowl of chicken soup at 4 o'clock. After that, we all rode back to school.

Comment

This is the first example in the course of narration story telling. The most common tense in narration is the past simple. This writing is also well organized. The first paragraph is the introduction and explanation. The second paragraph tells how to travel there. The third paragraph tells what happened there. The last paragraph tells later activities and how to travel back.

Look at the following example:

Example 2

A One-Day Trip

(Introduction and explanation)

I live in Beijing. Last week, I went to Beidaihe for a day with my family. Beidaihe is a seaside summer resort to the southeast of Beijing.

(Travelling there)

We got up very early and caught the train for Beidaihe at 7:00 a.m. We arrived in Beidaihe at about 10 o'clock in the morning.

(What happened there)

First we went to the beach. We played on the sand and then had a swim. Then we went to a restaurant and had a delicious lunch. After lunch, we walked along the coast. We visited a park and a museum. After that, we did some shopping. We bought some souvenirs.

(Travelling back)

At 5:30 p.m. we caught the train back to Beijing and got back home at 9 o'clock.

Exercise 3

Write about a day's outing you went on. Say who went with you, where you went and what you did.

The guide for the writing: (This guide may help you.)

(1) Introduction and explanation — who you are
                                 — where you live/lived
                                 — where you went
(2) Travelling there   — when you left
                                 — how you travelled
                                 — when you arrived
(3) What happened there   — what you did first
                                 — next
                                 — after that

	— when you had a meal
(4) Travelling back	— when you left
	— how you travelled
	— when you got back home

1.5. It is very common in narrative writing to write a simple personal narrative, relating the events of an important day in chronological order.

Read and study the following examples:

Example 1

The Day I Went to the Army Farm

Friday, the 11th of April, 1969, was an important day in my life. It was the day I went to the Army farm.

On Thursday evening, I said good-bye to my family and friends. I felt sad, but excited. I travelled by bus to the railway station. And then I got on the train. The journey was a very long one. I travelled all through the night from Beijing to Liu Zhao.

I arrived at the farm at six in the morning. I looked for the farming machines, but I did not see any. I felt very tired. I was taken to a small hut and given a bed. But I did not have time to sleep. A loud bell rang at seven. It was time for breakfast. After breakfast, we marched and queued for uniforms. Then we marched and queued for working tools. We marched and queued all day.

At the end of the day, I felt disappointed, tired and lonely. I had not seen any farming machines. I had marched all day. I had not liked anyone. I did not want to be on the Army farm. I wanted to go home. But I did not go home for three years.

Comment

The past perfect tense is used in this writing because it fits in naturally when narrating events in the past. Supperlative of adjectives and adjectival clauses are also used here. Adjective clauses are a very common feature in written English. The first paragraph of the writing is the introduction. The second paragraph tells the preparation and travel. The third paragraph tells the actual event. The last is the conclusion.

Look at example 2:

Example 2

The Day I Got my University Exam Results

Tuesday, July 22nd, 1989, was the most important day in my life. It was the day I got the results of my final examinations at the University of Edinburgh.

I got up early on that Tuesday morning and walked to the university. I met some friends there. They were also waiting for the results. We walked together to the examinations notice-board. The results were not up yet. A notice on the board said, "English Final Honours Results at 4:30 p.m."

It was then midday. We were very excited and we did not want to eat anything. We decided to go to the cinema. I do not remember anything about the film we saw. At 4 o'clock, we went back to the notice-board. The results had been put up. We all looked for our names. I soon saw mine. I had passed my finals.

All my friends had passed, too. That evening, there was a party and we celebrated our success. It was the happiest day of my life.

Exercise 4

Write about an important day or a very important day or the most important day in your life. Say what day it was and what happened on that day.

The guide for the writing: (This guide may help you.)

(1) Introduction	— the date
	— what happened
(2) Preparation and travel	— how you left
	— alone or with friends
	— travel
	— where
(3) The actual event	— what happened
	— morning
	— afternoon

                                                    — evening
          (4) Conclusion   — how the day ended
                                                    — how you felt

1.6. In academic writing, a narrative is often used to outline a sequence of steps
     carried out on a specific occasion. It is also particularly important in report-
     writing, when the writer outlines the developmental stages of an experiment
     or a piece of research, or the sequence of steps in an event such as a fire or an
     accident.

     Read the following example:

Example

Vicious Circle

     Malaria at one time infected 90% of the population of Borneo. In
1955, the World Health Organization began a DDT spraying programme
which virtually eliminated malaria. But other things began to happen. Besides killing mosquitoes, the DDT also killed other insects that lived in the
houses, such as flies and cockroaches. These insects were the favourite
food of geckos (small lizards). And so when the geckos ate the dead insects, they died from DDT poisoning. Similarly, the house cats ate the
dead geckos and cockroaches, and they too died from DDT poisoning. As a
result, the rat population rose sharply, and the human population of Bor-
neo began to die from a type of plague carried by fleas on the rats. In order
to deal with the emergency, thousands of cats were parachuted into the island, in what was called "Operation Cat Drop".

Comment

     This narrative outlines a sequence of steps carried out on a specific occasion.
This sequence of steps is in the exact order in which they took place. The simple
past tense is used here.

Exercise 5

     Outline a sequence of steps carried out on a specific occasion. Use simple past
tense in your writing.

     40

Read the following writing:

Example

The following experiment could be used to measure the ease of flow of the concrete.

The equipment needed consisted of a metal container in the shape of a truncated cone, a flat plate, a 16mm diameter rod and rule. The container had a diameter of 100mm at the closed end, 200mm at the other end and a height of 300mm.

Freshly mixed concrete made with aggregate of less than 50mm diameter was put into the cone in three layers. Each layer was compacted 25 times with the rod before the next layer was added. The cone was inverted over the plate and removed. The amount that the concrete settled or slumps showed its consistency.

Comment

This writing outlines the developmental stages of an experiment. The past passive is often used in this kind of writing as a narrative. When the present passive is used, it is often a description.

Exercise 6

Outline the developmental stages of an experiment or a piece of research. Use the past passive in your writing.

Read the following writing:

Example

It was raining heavily as the man was walking up the hill towards the station at 6 o'clock on a Saturday morning. At that early hour there wasn't much traffic and there weren't many people in sight. Just as the man was crossing the road near the top of the hill, a car came round the corner. It was travelling very fast and the driver was obviously having difficulty controlling it. Suddenly it swerved violently, skidded on the wet road, hit a lamp-post and turned over. The driver was unconscious and there was a lot of blood on his face. A young woman hurried into the station and phoned for an ambulance. A number of people gathered round the car, but there wasn't a great deal they could do. A policeman arrived a few minutes later and asked a lot of questions about the accident. Shortly afterwards the man came round, and he was groaning quietly when the ambulance arrived at high speed and rushed him away to the hospital.

Comment

This writing outlines the sequence of steps in a car accident. The simple past and the past continuous tenses are used in this narrative.

Exercise 7

Outline the sequence of steps in an event such as an accident or a fire. Use the simple past and past continuous tenses.

1.7. Vocabulary Guide

(1) now	(2) first	(3) previously
then	second	every day
next	third	a long time ago
before	once	one of these days
after	former	last year
subsequently	latter	up to this time
afterwards	before this/that	on the occasion
earlier	formerly	
later	prior to	
sooner		

(4) while	(5) yesterday	(6) finally
at the same time	the day before yesterday	eventually
meanwhile	two days ago	simultaneously
	tomorrow	in the end
	the day after tomorrow	at last
	in two days	

Exercise 8

1. Write the story of some event that you have experienced — a disaster, or a good

experience, or something humorous.

2. Imagine you have interviewed someone famous. Now write the story of his/her life.

3. Write a short account (150-200 words) of the stages of your education, mentioning (perhaps) the main things which you think you learnt at each stage.

4. Outline the developmental stages of an experiment or a piece of research.

2. Comparison and Contrast
（比较与对比）

Comparison and contrast is such a familiar everyday activity that it may be difficult for you to think of it as an important mental process. Comparison is the process of examining two or more things in order to establish their similarities, and contrast is the process of examining two or more things in order to establish their differences. Yet without the ability to perceive similarities, you could not classify, define, or generalize. And without the ability to perceive differences, you could not analyze, define, or describe.

2.1. In academic writing, there are basically two ways in which we can write essays that involve comparison and/or contrast. One way is to write down all the main points about one of the subjects to be compared, and then to take all the main points about the other subject, like this:

>   Introduction (includes thesis, sets up comparison)
>   Subject 1
>   Point 1
>   Point 2
>   Point 3
>
>   .
>
>   .
>
>   .
>
>   Subject 2
>   Point 1
>   Point 2
>   Point 3
>
>   .
>
>   .
>
>   .
>
>   Conclusion (summary, returns to beginning)

Example

The domestic hen, the hawk and the duck all belong to the bird category. They have some features in common such as wings, feet, beak, flight, nest, migration, food and eggs.

The domestic hen has short wings which it rarely uses because it has a heavy body and lives on the ground. It is clumsy in flight and can cover only short distances. Its feet are designed for scratching the ground to find seeds and worms. It will also eat almost any other kind of food. Hens nest on the ground. They have been bred for egg production and can lay up to 300 eggs a year.

Hawks have long, pointed, powerful wings for high, rapid flight. Their feet are designed to catch and grasp small birds and other small animals. Their beaks are sharp, for cutting up the animals they kill. They nest in trees and on high places. Hawks lay 3 to 6 eggs at a time and may lay twice a year.

A duck has webbed feet so that it can swim easily and walk on soft ground. It has a long, flat beak which it uses to search for food in river and pond mud. It has powerful wings which enable it to fly long distances. It nests in grass at the water's edge. Ducks migrate long distances. A duck lays 5 to 12 eggs at a time and may lay twice a year.

In conclusion, although there are something different among these three birds, the basic features are quite similar.

Exercise 1

1. Look at the following chart. Write down all the main points about the helicopter, and then take all the main points about the aeroplane.

FEATURE	HELICOPTER	AEROPLANE
propellers	rotor and tail	nose
wings	none	two
flight	all directions	forward only
take-off	vertical, no runway	runway needed

2. Study the following chart. Write down all the main points about the bicycle, and then take all the main points about the car.

FEATURE	BICYCLE	CAR
wheels	two	four
controls	human energy	uses petrol
speed	slow	fast
size	smaller	bigger

3. Prepare a chart for comparing and contrasting your country with any one of its neighbours. Your chart should list the key features to be compared and contrasted. Fill the chart, and then write a passage of comparison and contrast.

2.2. The other way in which we can write essays that involve comparison and/or contrast is to take each point in turn and contrast them immediately, like this:

Introduction (includes thesis, sets up comparison)

Subject 1		Subject 2
Point 1	to	Point 1
Point 2	to	Point 2
Point 3	to	Point 3
.		.
.		.
.		.

Conclusion (summary, returns to beginning)

Example 1

Cars and bicycles are similar in that they are both privately owned means of transport. In other words, they have in common the fact that the owner can decide when and where to go.

However, there are a lot of differences between them. A car costs a lot more to buy than a bicycle. In addition, it is far more expensive to run. For example, a car has to be insured, and must be serviced regularly; furthermore, spare parts for a car cost a lot of money. A car uses petrol, which is expensive, whereas a bicycle uses only human energy.

On the other hand, as far as comfort is concerned, a car is better than a bicycle. In a car you are protected from the weather, and have comfortable seats and plenty of room to carry people and luggage.

46

A car is not only more comfortable than a bicycle, it is faster as well.

With respect to convenience, it is difficult to say which one is better. A bicycle is certainly easier to park!

To sum up, each one has its advantages and disadvantages.

Example 2

Paintings and photographs have something in common. But, there are also some differences between them.

Paintings and photographs are visual art forms. They both can capture a specific moment for all time. A painting reflects the skill and talent of a painter, likewise the quality of a photograph can represent the skill and talent of a photographer.

Photographs are created by using film, a camera, and special paper. In contrast, paintings are created with paint, brushes, and canvas. Photographs, like paintings, are often framed and displayed on walls in homes and galleries. Both can vary in size. However, photographs are usually small enough to keep in albums where they document family events.

In conclusion, although paintings and photographs are similar in some ways, there are also some differences between them.

Comment

Example 1 compares and contrasts the two subjects point by point clearly in different paragraphs. The passage also can be organized into three paragraphs, like this:

Paragraph 1—Introduction
Paragraph 2— Comparison and/or Contrast
Paragraph 3—Conclusion

In example 2, the writer takes each point in turn, using one paragraph (second) comparing the similarities, and another paragraph (third) contrasting the differences.

Exercise 2

1. Write a passage to compare and/or contrast ballet dancers and football players. You should take each point in turn and compare or contrast them immediately.

(A sample writing is provided.)

2. There are two motorcycles. The Maxi is French, the Flexi is Italian. Here is some information about them. You are comparing or contrasting them for a magazine. Write a passage to show the good and bad points of each. You should take each point in turn and compare or contrast them immediately.

MAXI	FLEXI
very heavy	light
fast on hills	bad on hills
uncomfortable	comfortable to ride
good brakes	bad to start
double headlight	one headlight
reliable	difficult to lock
expensive	cheaper than average

2.3. Although similarity and difference are closely related, they can be regarded as being different mental processes. For example, in examining any two things, you can mentally explore their similarities without necessarily exploring their differences, or you can mentally investigate their differences without investigating their similarities.

Example 1

The city and the suburbs seem to be very different in many ways, but they also share many of the same problems, such as crime and drug addiction.

Crime is one problem found in both urban and suburban areas. Elderly people are mugged whether they are hurrying along a city street or strolling down a suburban avenue. Residents living in cities and suburbs hide in fear behind double-locked doors, hoping to prevent robberies. In both the cities and the suburbs, big, vicious dogs are used as additional protection against robberies. Even juvenile crime is a growing problem as gangs increase in the metropolitan and suburban areas.

Drug addiction is another problem shared by cities and suburbs. Young people growing up in overcrowded, unpleasant conditions in the city ghettoes often turn to drugs such as heroin for a temporary escape from life. Suburban youngsters turn to drug addiction to search for "kicks" and

48

to put excitement into their boring lives. Often they become addicted to another kind of drug—alcohol. Whether the drug is heroin, cocaine, or alcohol, it can be bought quite easily either in a city or on a suburban school playground. Parents and officials in both areas are worried by the prevalence of drug addiction.

To sum up, even though the cities and suburbs may still look different from each other, many problems facing these two areas today are really the same.

Example 2

There are many cultural differences between people of different societies, and sometimes these can lead to misunderstandings. Let us, for example, look at two common customs of smiling and giving gifts.

Firstly, there is smiling. In some societies people smile a lot, in others they don't. When it comes to laughing, the differences are even greater. In some places, it is quite common for people to laugh at misfortune. If someone falls and hurts himself, the people nearby may laugh. Or a person may laugh when telling someone about the death of a friend or a relative. In other societies, such behaviour seems shocking.

Then there is the custom of giving gifts. In Western societies, gifts are usually given on birthdays and at Christmas to one's relatives and close friends. These gifts should be opened in front of the person who is giving them, and that person should be thanked at that time. In some Eastern societies, on the other hand, birthdays are often ignored, and Christmas of course only affects the minority who are Christians, although Christmas cards seem to be becoming popular with many people who are not Christians. When gifts are given, they are usually put away, and very little is said about them.

These are only a few of many different ways in which different societies behave. It is important for people to understand such differences if they are going to have contact with each other without causing problems.

Comment

Example 1 mainly explores the similarities of the two problems between the city and the suburbs. And example 2 discusses some cultural differences between some countries. Both are very well organized.

Exercise 3

1. Write a passage to compare the similarities of the flow of electricity through wires and cables from the main supply and the flow of water through pipes from a water tank. (A sample writing is provided.)
2. Write a passage to contrast the differences between the northern and southern polar regions. (A sample writing is provided.)

2.4. Most of the examples of similarity and difference, thus far, have been concerned with expository prose. But comparison and contrast can also be the basis of argumentative prose. The following article is a good example of how comparison and contrast can be used to support an argument.

Example

When most people think about UFOs, they think of them as spaceships coming from outside the Earth, and manned by intelligent beings. Is there any chance of this? Do these beings really exist? There are arguments for and against this.

(for) Current theories about how life got its start make it seem that any planet with something like the Earth's chemistry and temperature would be sure to develop life. One reasonable estimate advanced by an astronomer was that there might be as many as 640,000,000 planets in our galaxy alone that are Earth-like and that bear life.

(against) Assuming there are 100 advanced civilization in our own galaxy and that they are evenly spread throughout the galaxy, the nearest one would be about 10,000 light-years away. Even assuming coverage of that distance at the fastest speed we know of —the speed of light — the trip would take at least 10,000 years. Why should anyone make such long journeys just to poke around curiously?

(for) It is wrong to try to estimate the abilities of a far-advanced civilization, or their motives either. For one thing, the situation may not be average. The nearest advanced civilization may just happen to be only 100 light-years away, rather than 10,000.

(against) But even if that were the case, it would make no sense to send so many spaceships so often (judging by the many UFO reports). Surely we are not that interesting. And if we are interesting, why not land

50

and greet us? Or communicate without landing? They can't be afraid of us, since if they are so far advanced beyond us, they can surely defend themselves against any of our puny threats.

J. A. Hynek, the most serious and level-headed investigator of UFOs, is a logical astronomer who is convinced that some UFO reports are worth serious investigation. He doesn't think they represent extraterrestrial spaceships, but he does suggest that they represent phenomena that lie outside the present structure of science, and that understanding them will help us expand our knowledge and build a greatly enlarged structure of science.

Comment

The organizational pattern of this article is very pronounced. The writer sets up his thesis in the first paragraph —the introduction paragraph —("Do these beings really exist?") and then uses the last sentence in that paragraph to organize the essay ("There are arguments for and against this."). Then in subsequent paragraphs, he takes up one point at a time, explores it thoroughly, and then considers a contrasting point of view. The resultant pattern is for/against, for/against, followed by a conclusion.

In this article, the writer dispassionately analyzes the question as to whether life exists on other planets. He presents evidence and logical reasoning, refuting each argument point by point, but he does this within the framework of a comparison paradigm. He tries to convince his readers intellectually, by conviction rather than by emotional appeal, and each step in the process is clearly formulated. Conviction is the logical part of argument that avoids the shaky emotional basis of some persuasive argument. In IELTS, due to time limitation, the best pattern is just one pair of for/against.

Exercise 4

Write essays on the following topics. Use the for/against pattern.
Topic 1: Discuss the question of the death penalty in general. How far do you think it is justified?
Topic 2: Some people purchase a home and others rent. Describe one or two benefits of owning a home and one or two benefits of renting. Compare the two options and explain which you think might be better for overseas students.
(Both topics are provided with sample writings.)

2.5. In most academic subjects, and in life generally, we often need to compare and contrast things. Tables, charts and graphs are useful in presenting information of comparison and contrast. Examine the following table, chart and graph, then read the sample writing.

(1) Examine the following table:

Age of car (years)	Make A			Make B		
	Petrol consumption	Re-liability	N	Petrol consumption	Re-liability	N
1	√√	√	26	XX	X	22
2	X	√√	82	O	X	44
3	√	√	110	X	X	25
4	O	√	91	O	X	22
5	√	√	58	X	O	19

Key: √√ = much better than average performance
√ = better than average performance
O = average performance
X = worse than average performance
XX = much worse than average performance

Note: If a car has a better performance in the tests on its petrol consumption, we would say that it is (very) *economical* to run.

Sample writing:

This table shows the performance of two makes of cars, designated A and B, in tests to determine their petrol consumption and reliability. The cars were between the ages of 1 and 5 years. The size of the sample is indicated in the column marked N and the key explains the symbols used.

The results show a clear difference in the petrol consumption and reliability of the two makes of cars. With two exceptions, Make A was consistently more economical and reliable than the average, whereas Make B was, with three exceptions, less reliable than average. Therefore, on the evidence available, Make A would seem more economical and reliable than Make B.

However it should be noted that the Make A sample was almost three times as large as the Make B sample, and it is therefore possible that a larger sample of Make B cars would provide very different results.

It is also interesting to note that in neither case was there a significant correlation between the age of the car and its performance in the tests.

Comment

In this writing there are four paragraphs. Two of the paragraphs compare results, one introduces the results and explains how they are set out, and one gives a warning about the results. Some comparative expressions are used, such as: *more... than ...*; *less ... than ...*; *as ... as*. This writing is also a good example of report writing.

(2) Examine the following chart:

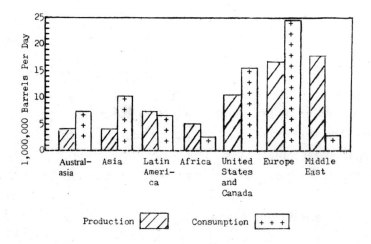

Sample writing:

This chart of world petroleum consumption compared to petroleum production shows a tremendous difference among regions. Some use more than they produce, while others produce more than they use. Certain regions have large petroleum production but lack the industry and transportation to utilize it. They are able to make a profit by selling to regions that need it.

Four regions shown consume more petroleum than they produce. Both Australia and Asia consume about fifty percent more than they produce. Europe consumes about seventy-five percent more than it produces. The United States and Canada together produce about three fifths of what they consume.

53

Three regions shown on the chart produce more than they consume. Latin America produces approximately ten percent more than it consumes. Africa produces more than twice what it consumes, and the Middle East is the biggest producer of all.

The United States, Canada, and Europe use a great deal more than they produce, but each produces a considerable amount. The high consumption probably results from their industrial and transportation requirements. On the other hand, Africa and the Middle East produce much more than they use, which probably indicates low petroleum needs in industry and transportation.

As the chart describes, certain regions produce more petroleum than they consume, and others consume more than they produce. Those with a surplus can profit by selling it to the large consumers that cannot produce all that they need.

Comment

In this writing there are five paragraphs. The first is the introduction and the last is the conclusion. In the body of the writing, the writer shows the information in groups in stead of one by one. One group talks about the regions which consume more petroleum than they produce. The other group shows the opposite. One paragraph (the fourth paragraph) gives the reasons why some regions consume more than they produce and some other regions produce more than they consume.

(3) Examine the following graph:

The changes in the popularity of cinema and television 1957–1974

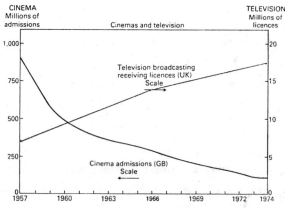

Sample writing:

The above graph shows the changes in the popularity of cinema and

54

television between 1957 and 1974.

According to the graph, over the period from 1957 to 1974 the trend was towards a decrease in the popularity of the cinema. There was a dramatic fall in the number of cinema admissions from 1957, when about 900 million people went, to 1959, when the attendance figure was roughly 550 million. From 1959 to 1963 the rate of decrease slowed down, the figure for the latter year being about 350 million. From this year on, there was a more gradual reduction in the popularity of the cinema, reaching a figure of about 125 million in 1974.

There was an upward trend in the number of TV licences issued in this period. In 1957 about 7 million licences were issued, and this figure rose steadily, reaching 14 million in 1966, to a peak of 17 million in 1974.

One of the reasons less people went to the cinema and more people stayed at home to watch television was probably because people tried to have more privacy and comfort.

Exercise 5

Write comparative and/or contrasting passages on the following topics:

(1) The table below shows the concentration of smoke in different parts of Britain in two different periods. The smoke concentration is measured in micrograms per cubic metre. Begin by describing the situation and then write out your comparison. Try to draw some conclusions, if you can.
(A sample writing is provided.)

AREA	1969~70	1971~72
The North of England	95%	80%
The Northwest of England	90%	70%
The West Midlands of England	54%	48%
The Southwest of England	31%	30%
Scotland	79%	44%
Wales	32%	38%

(2) Look at the population graphs below and write out your comparison in the form of paragraphs, and try to draw some conclusions, if you can. Begin by describing the situation in present-day Sweden, and then go on to compare present-day Sweden with the data from 200 years earlier.
(A sample writing is provided.)

The Population Graphs

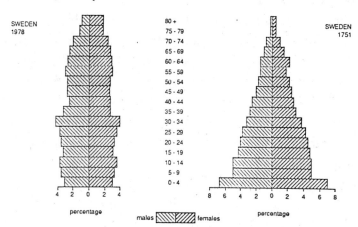

(3) Write out your comparison according to the information given in the following graphs.

(A sample writing is provided.)

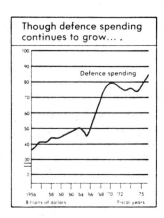

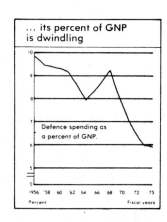

2.6. As we can see, when studying tables and other statistical information, the language of comparison and contrast is frequently needed. This section tries to help the candidates gain a better knowledge of 1) formation of the regular and irregular comparative and superlative of adjectives and adverbs; and 2) basic sentence patterns used in comparison and contrast.

2.6.1. Formation of the regular and irregular comparative and superlative of adjectives and adverbs.

A. The regular comparative and superlative of adjectives and adverbs is formed as follows:

a. by adding the endings -er and -est. E.g.

old — older, oldest

soon — sooner, soonest

56

b. by placing the words "more" and "most" in front of words usually with more than two syllables. E.g.

important — more important, most important

easily — more easily, most easily

Note: When a superlative is used, the definite article "the" is often put before it. E.g.

the most interesting

the oldest

B. Irregular comparison is made up of a small group of very frequently used adjectives and adverbs. E.g.

adjectives:

> good — better, best
> bad — worse, worst
> many — more, most
> far — further (farther), furthest (farthest)

adverbs:

> well — better, best
> badly — worse, worst
> much — more, most
> little — less, least

2.6.2. Basic sentence patterns used in comparison and contrast.

A. When the similarities need to be pointed out in comparison, the following sentence patterns can be used:

a. the same ... as/the same as ...

E.g.

A is the same weight as B.

A weighs the same as B.

b. as ... as

E.g.

A is as heavy as B.

c. to be similar to ... in ...

E.g.

A is similar to B in height.

d. in common

E.g.

A and B have the height in common.

B. When the differences need to be pointed out in contrast, the following sentence patterns can be used:

a. comparative + than ...

   E.g.

     B is less expensive than A.

b. to be different from/ to differ from

   E.g.

     B is different from A in price.

     B differs from A in price.

C. When more than two things are compared, the following sentence pattern can be used:

the + superlative

E.g.

     C is the lightest of the three.

     C weighs the least.

Exercise 6

1. Fill in the missing forms:

POSITIVE	COMPARATIVE	SUPERLATIVE
Example: good	better	best
(1) anxiously		
(2) cautiously		
(3) cold		
(4) dirty		
(5) easily		
(6) grandly		
(7) plain		
(8) quickly		
(9) simple		
(10) straight		
(11) slow		
(12) careful		
(13) late		
(14) seriously		
(15) speedy		
(16) beautiful		
(17) safe		
(18) light		
(19) colourful		

(20) skillful

2. Fill in the blanks with the appropriate forms of the words given in parentheses:
   (1) (young) Tom is the ... of the three children.
   (2) (hot) It is ... today than it was yesterday.
   (3) (old, young) A is eighteen years old; B is nineteen and C is twenty-one.
       A is the ... and C is the .... B is ... than A, but ... than C.
   (4) (old) My sister is three years ... than I am. She is the ... among us.
   (5) (large) Guangzhou is ... than any other city in South China.
   (6) (large) Xinjiang is the ... province in China. It is sixteen times as ... as
       Zhejiang.
   (7) (good) I want to buy a ... fountain pen. Show me some ... ones you
       have. Oh, this one is ... than that.
   (8) (well) He was not feeling ... when I saw him last. He is feeling ...
       now.
   (9) (near) Where is the ... post-office?
   (10) (large; small) Suzhou is not as ... as Shanghai. Suzhou is .... .
   (11) (old) The ... Greek legend celebrated chariot racing.
   (12) (much) A king loved one of his daughters ... of all.
   (13) (worthy) Each young suitor was ... than the last.
   (14) (noble) Still he forbade even the ... man he had ever met.
   (15) (skillful) Could any of them be a ... driver than the president?
   (16) (confidently) He ... challenged twelve to a race.
   (17) (beautiful) The princess was the ... woman in the kingdom.
   (18) (deeply) She had fallen ... in love with Tom.
   (19) (fast) Mary drove ... than Tom.
   (20) (little) He had ... trouble than the other students.

2.7. Structure and Vocabulary Aid: Qualification of Comparison

(1) X is

considerably	smaller than Y.	
much	bigger	
a lot	cheaper	
somewhat	etc.	
a bit		
a little		
slightly		
hardly		
only just		

(2) X is   exactly   the same as Y.
               precisely
               just
               practically
               more or less
               almost
               nearly
               approximately
               about

(3) X is not   exactly   the same as Y.
               entirely
               quite

(4) X is not quite as/so big   as Y.
               expensive
               dear
               etc.

(5) X is   totally   different from Y.
               completely
               entirely
               quite

(6) X and Y are   different   in every   way.
               dissimilar   respect.

       X and Y are   totally   different.
               completely
               entirely
               quite

3. Cause and Effect
(原因与结果)

3.1. A cause is what makes something happen. An effect is what happens because of the cause. In discussing cause and effect we are discussing why things happen. For example:

(1) Mary ran to the station because she wanted to catch the train.

In sentence (1), (*Mary*) *wanted to catch the train* is the cause; *ran to the station* is the effect. Look at more sentences:

(2) Because Tom overslept, he rushed to school without eating breakfast.

(3) Lili checked her alarm clock carefully, so tomorrow she will awaken on time and will not be late for school.

(4) Because Mary loves ice-skating and practises daily, she is winning many competitions.

In sentence (2), *Tom overslept* is the cause; *he rushed to school* is the effect. Sentences (3) and (4) are different. In sentence (3), *checked her alarm clock carefully* is the cause; *will awaken on time tomorrow and will not be late for school* are two effects. In sentence (4), *loves ice-skating and practises daily* are two causes; *is winning many competitions* is the effect.

In practice, some writers will sometimes tend to stress cause (like sentence (2)); at other times, they may place the chief emphasis upon effect (like sentence (1)). One cause can produce more than one effect (like sentence (3)), and one effect can have more than one cause (like sentence (4)).

Exercise 1

Identify the cause and the effect in each sentence. Remember that a sentence may have more than one cause or effect.

Example: I didn't study enough, so I failed the test.

Answer: cause: didn't study enough

effect: failed the test

(1) Mary believed that her slender diet resulted in long life.

cause: _____

effect: _____

(2) The extreme cold causes the ice to freeze and glaciers to form.

cause: _____

effects: _____

(3) Overeating and the flu will lead to stomachache.

causes: _____

effect: _____

(4) Too much sun brings about headache and sunburn.

cause: _____

effects: _____

(5) Because of his depression, he overate.

cause: _____

effect: _____

(6) The war started because the economic situation was desperate.

effect: _____

cause: _____

(7) Since we carried plenty of water on the hike, we weren't thirsty.

cause: _____

effect: _____

(8) Pulmonary lesions are due almost entirely to the human form of the tubercle bacillus.

effect: _____

cause: _____

(9) He missed his flight owing to a traffic hold-up.

effect: _____

cause: _____

(10) Drunkenness results from too much alcohol.

effect: _____

cause: _____

(11) The soil erosion is the result of heavy rain and strong winds.

effect: _____

causes: _____

(12) The drought is the effect of lack of rain.

effect: _____

cause: _____

(13) As a result of drought, the crops were ruined.

cause: _____

effect: _____

(14) Lung cancer may be caused by cigarette smoking.

cause: _____

effect: _____

(15) Mary was late for her first class, so she got a tardy slip.

cause: _____

effect: _____

(16) The bus was held up by the snowstorm, thus causing the delay.

cause: _____

effect: _____

(17) The land absorbs heat from the sun, and therefore the air above it becomes hot.

cause: _____

effect: _____

(18) He was out of health, consequently he could not go to school.

cause: _____

effect: _____

(19) The computer has become smaller and cheaper and hence more available to a greater number of people.

cause: _____

effect: _____

(20) The heated air expands and rises. As a result, an area of low pressure forms over the land.

causes: _____

effect: _____

(Check the key at the back of this book.)

Comment

Understanding cause-and-effect relationships helps you understand what you read. The event before the words and phrases such as *to result in*, *to cause*, *to lead to*, *to bring about* is usually the CAUSE. (See items 1 to 4.) The event after the words and phrases such as *because of*, *because*, *since*, *to be due to*, *owing to*, *to result from*, *to be the result of*, *to be the effect of*, *as a result of*, *to be caused by* is usually the CAUSE. (See items 5 to 14.) The event after the words and phrases such as *so*, *thus*, *therefore*, *consequently*, *hence*, *as a result* is usually the EFFECT. (See items 15 to 20.) *Thus* is a fairly formal word. You use *thus* to show that what you are about to mention is the result or consequence of something else that you have just mentioned.

Hence is a formal word. You use *hence* to indicate that you have just given a reason for what you are about to say.

When an effect may have several causes or a cause several effects, you add *may*. (See item 14.)

Exercise 2

1. Look at the following lists. Items on the left can be causes or effects of items on the right. But the items are mixed up. Join the items on the left with the correct items on the right by using necessary words or phrases provided.

Example: 1. Prices rose (as a result)   a. the strike
          2. Bad labour conditions (caused) b. fewer goods were sold
Answer: 1. Prices rose. As a result, fewer goods were sold.
         2. Bad labour conditions caused the strike.

(1) Any marks on the leaves are probably (due to)...	a. he worked hard
(2) There is acid in that bottle, and (therefore)...	b. prolonged illness
	c. it must be handled very carefully
(3) Delayed treatment aften (results in)...	d. the same virus
(4) He passed his examination (because)...	e. her husband came home late and didn't call
(5) The accident occurred (because of)...	f. he fell off his bike
(6) Bad labour relations (caused)...	g. the strike
(7) Bill scraped his knee (because)...	h. the icy road conditions
(8) Mary was worried (because)...	i. the new seedlings have died
(9) A rise in incomes will create increased purchasing power, (thus)...	j. the insect escaped
(10) Tom broke his leg, and (therefore)...	k. he couldn't play in the game
(11) Mary forgot to put the top on the grasshopper's box, (consequently),...	l. stimulating demand for goods and services
(12) (Since) it has not rained in several days...	m. heart disease
(13) Tom left the headlights on last night, (hence)...	n. we fed it
(14) The kitten looked very thin, (so)...	o. the car won't start
(15) Smoking (may cause)...	

64

2. Fill in the blanks to complete each statement:

Example: It rained all day today, consequently, _____.
Answer: It rained all day today, consequently, we didn't play basketball.

(1) Our air conditioner is broken, as a result, _____.
(2) The library was closed, and therefore, _____.
(3) We had a flat tire, consequently, _____.
(4) There was a tremendous storm. Because of it, _____.
(5) I didn't have any stamps, so _____.
(6) I fell and twisted my ankle because of _____.
(7) _____, and therefore, I'm not going to the party.
(8) _____, consequently, I couldn't complete my homework.
(9) A piece of iron was left in the rain. Thus. _____.
(10) An increased percentage of home ownership was one effect of _____ during the 80's.

3.2. Cause-and-effect essays tend to fall into two basic types: those in which you proceed from cause to effect and those in which you move from effect to cause. Cause and effect sequences fall into relatively simple patterns.

3.2.1. Cause-to-Effect Pattern

Introduction (includes thesis)
Cause
Effect 1
Effect 2

.

.

.

Conclusion (summary and so forth)

Example

A few years ago, the United States sold millions of bushels of corn and wheat to the Soviet Union. At that time, some critics advocated that Americans should drink less in order to make more grain available for food.

That idea went over like a lead balloon with the liquor industry. They argued that only a small amount of grain, comparatively speaking, goes into the production of hard liquor. Eliminating booze production, they maintained, would make very little difference in the food supply. Now, a few years later, prospects for a record grain production are so good that these critics have been silenced, and liquor consumers may look forward to some relief from the higher prices.

The Agriculture Department estimates the 1975 corn crop will yield a record 6.05 billion bushels. Farmers are delighted at what they expect to be a record harvest. Already over 177 million bushels of corn have been sold to the Soviet Union, and the Agriculture Department expects corn exports to exceed 1 billion bushels.

One effect of this projected record harvest is expected to be lower prices for whiskey drinkers and drinkers of other kinds of alcoholic spirits, although one liquor industry spokesman maintains that a record grain crop would have a negligible effect on whiskey prices. It would, however, keep prices from going up.

Another effect of a bumper corn harvest would be that the cost of livestock grain would go down, thus resulting in lower prices for milk, meat, and poultry.

Whiskey imbibers are being warned, however, not to cheer too soon. Some critics are complaining that the recent grain deal with Russia could send prices skyrocketing again.

Comment

This writing is based on a very simple cause-to-effect pattern. The opening paragraph provides the introduction, giving the reader some background concerning fluctuating prices for grain and liquor prices. The second paragraph states the cause for a possible reduction in liquor and food prices. Paragraphs 3 and 4 give the effects of a bumper grain harvest: lower liquor prices and lower food prices. And the last paragraph concludes with a warning.

Exercise 3

For the last hundred years the world climate has been growing much warmer. Owing to this cause, it leads to a number of different effects. Write an essay, following the cause-to-effect pattern as explained above.

(A sample writing is provided.)

3.2.2. Effect-to-Cause Pattern

Introduction (includes thesis)
Effect
Cause 1
Cause 2

.
.
.

Conclusion (summary and so forth)

Example

Transmalia is a small place in West Africa—in the rainy part where there is dense tropical forest. One of its main problems is in the north where yellow fever is endemic and in most villages there is a number of cases each year.

The problem of controlling the disease is made difficult by several reasons. First, many of the people who live in the north are nomads who wander across the borders of neighbouring countries, which makes it almost impossible to check on the whole population.

Second, the disease is due to a virus which is transmitted to man by mosquitoes. It is impossible for a man to stay in a mosquito net throughout the whole day. He has to walk from here to there. This takes the chances. Epidemics take place during the hot season which is just the reproductive period of mosquitoes.

These two are the main reasons of the problem of controlling the disease though there are some others. Some possible measures have been already under consideration.

Comment

This writing is based on the effect-to-cause pattern. The opening paragraph provides the introduction. Then the writer follows the usual way and states the event (the problem of controlling the disease) in the second paragraph. After this, he explicitly spells out two causes, followed by the conclusion.

Exercise 4

1. There is a gradual reduction in the popularity of the cinema. Write an essay to

show the likely causes.

2. The Chinese government spent a lot of money sending a large number of scholars and students to study abroad. Some of them planned not to return. Provide some possible causes of this effect.

3. There is a tendency that the average age of marriage is getting earlier in some parts of the countryside. Give likely causes of these early marriages.

3.3. The basic purpose of a cause-and-effect paragraph or essay is to explain why a condition exists. Although some causes and effects are so complex that they require an entire paper to explain, simpler cause-and-effect relationships can often be explained within a single paragraph. Read the following paragraphs. Note the causes (why something happened) and effects (what happened).

Paragraph 1

The decision to keep a pet can cause a major change in a family's lifestyle. Since pets require attention, family members have to be willing to give up some of their free time to care for them. Pets depend on people to keep them clean, well fed, and healthy. Therefore, families must arrange to have someone care for the animal when they go away on vacation, and, if the animal is sick, take it to the vet. If a dog is selected as a pet, time has to be set aside for walking and exercising it. Pets are fun but helpless, and consequently, are a big responsibility to a family.

Paragraph 2

Cats were not always as popular as they are today. During the Middle Ages, some people in certain parts of the world thought cats were evil. As a result, cats were feared and persecuted. Consequently, the population of rats and mice grew in the cities because there were not enough cats to hunt them. Today, cats are sometimes kept because they hunt mice, but mostly because they are good company.

Exercise 5

Identify the causes and effects in paragraphs 1 and 2 above. Underline the causes and parenthesize the effects.

Example: The decision to keep a pet can cause (a major change in a family's lifestyle).

3.4. Cause and effect is related to narration and to process because all three are concerned with chronological progression. But in cause and effect, you are more interested in the WHY than in the WHAT or the HOW. Cause and effect exposition is a special form of exposition that presents a step by step description of associated sequences of events. Something more than just contiguity is involved in the process.

Read the following examples:

Example 1

The Erosion of the Land Caused by Rivers and Glaciers

When rain falls on mountains, it collects in depressions in the rock. The extreme cold causes the ice to freeze and glaciers to form. The ice melts and freezes again due to changes in temperature. Erosion of the rock of the mountain depression occurs as a result of the continual melting and refreezing, and is increased by the action of wind moving the water. Eventually, the water wears away the rock enough to form a small stream which carries deposits of soil and rock which cause further erosion, gradually enlarging the stream bed. The weather, too, acts on rocks and soil – to split, break and wear away. The stream grows larger until eventually it reaches the old age stage. The silt from the river is deposited into the sea, resulting in sandbars, spits and promontories.

Example 2

Inflation

Inflation is a process of steadily rising prices, resulting in a diminishing of the purchasing power of a given nominal sum of money. In other words, you can buy fewer goods for one pound in December than you could in January of the same year.

One type of inflation is known as supply-demand inflation. This occurs under conditions of full employment, when demand exceeds supply of goods, that is to say, when people want to buy more goods than are available.

The process of supply-demand inflation operates as follows. An increased demand for goods leads to an increased demand for labour, resulting in higher wages and salaries. This has the effect of increasing costs of production and thus causes increased prices.

69

However, as wages and salaries are higher, the increased demand for goods continues, and so the cycle of inflation goes on.

Exercise 6

1. Write a short passage to explain why the wind blows from the sea to the land during the day. (A sample writing is provided.)
2. Write a short passage to explain why some plants become sickly or die. (A sample writing is provided.)

3. 5. Vocabulary Guide

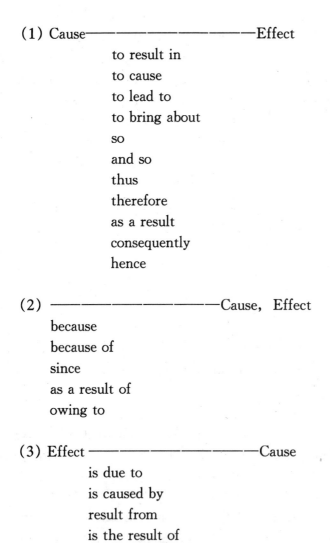

    (1) Cause————————————Effect

            to result in
            to cause
            to lead to
            to bring about
            so
            and so
            thus
            therefore
            as a result
            consequently
            hence

    (2) ————————————Cause, Effect

    because
    because of
    since
    as a result of
    owing to

    (3) Effect ————————————Cause

            is due to
            is caused by
            result from
            is the result of
            is the effect of

3.6. Degree of Certainty

When discussing cause and effect, we often want to show how sure we are about the relationship, i.e. the degree of certainty. The following chart is a rough guide to how we express this:

PERCENTAGE	FREQUENCY	CERTAINTY	VERB
100%	always	certainly	will
		undoubtedly	must
			simple present tense
	almost always		should
	usually		ought to
	most of the time		
	frequently		
	generally		
	as a rule		
	often	probably	
	many a time	likely	
50%	half of the time	presumably	
	sometimes	possibly	can
	occasionally	perhaps	could
	once in a while		may
			might
	seldom	unlikely	
	rarely		
	hardly ever		
0%	never		will not
			cannot
			could not
			simple present tense (negative)

71

4. Description
（描述）

Description is a mental process, a way of perceiving objects in space and time. As it pertains to composition, description is a way of picturing images verbally in speech or writing and of arranging those images in logical or associational pattern.

Generally, description is concerned with people, places and things. But in academic writing, especially in IELTS, you have to write a simple description of an object, a process or some data. According to this requirement, two writing techniques are mainly concerned in IELTS when writing a description. They are: static description and process description.

4.1. Static Description（静物描述）

Very often we have to describe the appearance or layout of something. We shall refer to this as static description. In IELTS, you may be required to write a description about an aerosol container, a camera or a microwave oven. When describing such things a number of features may be mentioned: shape, size, colour, location of parts and condition. Usually in writing static description the following principles should be observed:

(1) Your description should be well organised, e.g. general to particular, more important to less important, front to back, top to bottom, etc.
(2) You should offer the reader a clear picture in his mind of what you are describing.
(3) The details must be correct.
(4) You should stick to the important parts.

Read the following examples:

Example 1

A Water Clock

A water clock mainly consists of three parts which are a kind of tank, a container and a cylinder. The tank on the left holds water. This tank has a very narrow opening at the bottom on the right, and the water drips through this opening into the container which is in the middle. This container has an object which floats in it and the end of this is attached to a long pole with an arrow at the end. On the right there is a cylinder with the numbers one to twelve written on it.

Example 2

A Relay

A relay is a switching device for opening and closing one or more electrical circuits on receipt of an electrical signal.

A simple kind of relay consists of two parts: a switch in a high voltage circuit which is operated by a spring loaded armature and a low voltage electro-magnetic circuit.

The electro-magnet comprises a soft iron core shaped like a horseshoe. Each arm of the core has a coil wound around it. The coils are connected to each other and to a battery through an on/off switch.

In writing static description, the following words are quite useful:

above	在……上
below	在……下
over	在……上
underneath	在……下
at the front	在前部
at the back	在后部
to the left	在左部
to the right	在右部
on the left-hand side	在左手边
on the right-hand side	在右手边
in the middle	在中间
near	近
close to	靠近
apart	相隔
some distance from	相隔一段距离
upper	上面的
higher	更高的
lower	更低的
on top of	在……上面

at the top of 在……上部
at the foot of 在……底部
at the base of 在……底部
at the bottom of 在……底部
beside 在……旁边
alongside 在……旁边
on one side 在一边
on the other side 在另一边
front 前面
back 后面
rear 后面
upside down 颠倒的
inverted 颠倒的
inside 里面的
within 在……里面
outside 外面的
to be shaped like 形状像……
to be attached to 与……相连
circle 圆形
square 方形
triangle 三角形
rectangle 长方形
straight line 直线
sloping line 斜线
horizontal line 水平线
vertical line 垂直线
hyperbolic curve 曲线

Exercise 1

1. Write a short passage to describe a dry battery.
   (A sample writing is provided.)
2. Write a short paragraph to describe a spray aerosol container.
   (A sample writing is provided.)
3. Write a description of an electric motor.
   (A sample writing is provided.)

4.2. Process Description (过程描述)

A process is a series of actions, changes, functions, steps, stages, procedures, or operations that bring about a particular end or result. Like narration, process suggests ongoing movement and continuous action. The rhetorical structure of a process may be conveyed by a very simple pattern:

Introduction (thesis)
Step (or stage) 1
Step (or stage) 2
Step (or stage) 3
.
.
.

Conclusion (summary and so forth)

Read the following example:

Example

How a Television Broadcast is Made of a Football Game

Cameras and microphones are used for television broadcasting, and a television broadcast usually consists of four stages.

At the first stage several cameras are used. Each camera gives a different picture of the game. At the same time, a commentator describes the game. The commentator speaks into a microphone.

At the second stage, a television camera changes (converts) the picture into electric signals. These electric signals (vision signals) are sent to the television studio centre. The microphone converts the sound into another set of electric signals (sound signals). These sound signals are also sent to the television studio centre.

After this, at the studio centre, the producer watches the pictures from each camera and listens to the commentator. He chooses the best picture. Then the programme is sent out from the television centre.

Finally, the sound and vision signals are sent to the transmitting station.

This is how a television broadcast is made of a football game.

Comment

Usually, and from the example as well, we can see that the emphasis in a process theme, however, is on the HOW, rather than the WHAT. In academic writing, two very common kinds of process description are describing   1) how to do something, and   2) how something works.

4.2.1. Describing How to Do Something

In describing how to do something the main thing is to arrange the information so that the process can be done straight through without unnecessary interruptions. The description should be moving forward in a logical, step-by-step sequence. In order to show how the ideas are connected, some useful conjunctions or links are used.

Read the following examples:

Example 1

How to Sort Letters

First of all, letters and packets are collected in bags from pillar boxes, post offices and firms, in post office vans. They are then taken to the sorting office, where the bags are emptied and the letters separated from the packets. Following this step, the letters are put through machines so that the stamps can be cancelled. In this process the date and place of sorting are put over the stamps on each envelope. In the next stage, the sorting of the letters takes place, according to the county they are addressed to. This is done by placing them in the appropriate pigeon hole. Subsequently, the letters are taken from the pigeon holes and placed in baskets, which are then put onto a conveyor belt. While on this conveyor belt, the baskets are directed to the appropriate secondary sorting section by means of coding pegs. At the secondary sorting frames, the letters are put into towns in the county. Later, the letters are tied in bundles and a label is put on showing the towns they are addressed to. Finally, the letter bundles are placed in bags, which have the post office seal, post office railway number and destination code number on them, and then these are sent to the railway station.

Example 2

How to Make a Record

There are many different steps in the making of a record. Here is a description of the process that brings records into the shops.

The musicians play and sing. The sound they make is picked up by the microphones (about 16 — 20 of them).

The sounds are changed into electricity and sent through wires to the mixer, where they are made louder or quieter.

The signals are then sent to the tape recorder, which records them on to 16 tracks on the tape. All the instruments are kept separate.

Afterwards, the recordings are mixed again, and a new tape is made, with only two tracks (stereo). Some sounds are placed on the "left" of the tape, so they can be heard from the left loudspeaker.

This stereo tape is taken to the cutting machine. This cuts a groove into a piece of metal. Two pieces of metal are cut—one for Side One and one for Side Two of the record.

This metal disc with grooves is then used to make another metal disc—with ridges.

From this metal disc (called a father) a steel disc with grooves is made. This is called a mother. It is played by the engineers, and the sound quality is checked.

From the mother, two son discs are made, and are put into a pressing machine with some black plastic in the middle.

The press is heated, and the plastic melts and flows between the ridges of the metal discs. So a plastic record is made, with grooves cut into each of its sides. This is cooled with water and taken out.

The record is put into a sleeve and sent to the record shop.

Vocabulary guide: useful conjuctions or links

firstly　首先
first of all　首先
to begin with　首先
the first step is...　第一步是……
the first stage is...　第一阶段是……
at the first stage　在第一阶段

secondly　第二

next　其次；然后

then　然后；接着

subsequently　随后

after this　此后

the next step is...　下一步是……

in the next stage　在下一阶段中

in the following stage　在下面的阶段中

at the same time　同时

simultaneously　同时

finally　最后

eventually　最后

the last step is...　最后一步是……

in the last stage　在最后一阶段中

Exercise 2

1. Write a passage to describe how to develop a film.
   (A sample writing is provided.)
2. Write a passage to describe how to mend a flat bicycle tyre.
   (A sample writing is provided.)
3. Write a passage to describe how to make paper.
   (A sample writing is provided.)

4.2.2. Describing How Something Works

In describing how something works, the procedure is very similar to the other kind of description. The description must be orderly, step by step. The basic principle involved should be described. The basic principle must be clearly understood, otherwise the details will just confuse the reader.

Read the following examples:

Example 1

How a Microwave Oven Works

A microwave oven will cook food much more quickly than an ordinary gas or electric cooker.

In a conventional oven, infra-red heat is used to warm the food and the heat travels from the outside inwards. The microwave oven uses radiation waves. These waves cause the molecules making up the food to vibrate. This vibration leads to friction between the molecules and it is this friction that causes the food to heat up and cook. Microwaves are electromagnetic radiation that has an ultra-high frequency (UHF). The radiation is produced by means of an electronic tube called a magnetron.

In a typical microwave oven, the waves of energy are beamed along a metal tube called a waveguide to a stirrer. The stirrer acts like a fan. It is driven by a motor and distributes the energy evenly over the food being cooked.

Metal containers are not used in microwave ovens, since they deflect the microwave energy which might damage the magnetron. However non-metallic materials such as paper, plastic and ceramics do not absorb microwave energy and do not, therefore, become hot. Thus they make excellent containers for cooking food in.

Example 2

How a Blast Furnace Works

Smelting of iron ore takes place in a blast furnace. At the beginning of the process the furnace is charged with coke (C), iron ore (Fe_2O_3) and limestone ($CaCO_3$), which are placed in alternate layers. Then a blast of hot air at high pressure enters through the tuyere at the bottom of the furnace. At this stage the coke burns to form carbon dioxide. As the hot carbon dioxide rises in the furnace, it meets more hot coke and is reduced to carbon monoxide. The carbon monoxide then reacts with the hot iron ore, forming iron and carbon dioxide. At the same time, the limestone absorbs earthy impurities from the ore, forming a liquid known as slag.

The molten iron and liquid slag drain to the bottom of the furnace, where they form two layers – the slag floats on top of the denser molten iron. The molten crude iron and slag pass out of the furnace at different levels. The main product of a blast furnace is known as pig or crude iron.

Exercise 3

1. Write a passage to describe how a camera works.

(A sample writing is provided.)
2. Write a passage to describe how a refrigerator works.
(A sample writing is provided.)

4.2.3. Cyclical Process

The process of describing how to do something and how something works usually has a clear beginning and an end. There is another kind of process often used in academic writing which is cyclical process. In a cyclical process there is no clear beginning or end, so that the cycle is continuously repeated.

Look at the following diagram which illustrates the nitrogen cycle. And then study the example.

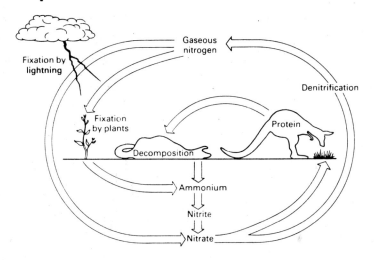

Example

This diagram illustrates the nitrogen cycle. Nitrogen is essential for human, animal and plant life, and over 90% of the earth's supply exists as a gas in the atmosphere. The diagram shows how nitrogen is provided to living organisms and then returned to the atmosphere.

The cycle goes like this. The lightning contributes some nitrogen, in the form of nitrates, to the soil. The nitrates in the soil are absorbed by plant roots. When animals eat the plants, the nitrogen they contain is synthesized into protein. When plants or animals die, proteins are decomposed by bacteria into amino acids which are in turn broken down into ammonium. The ammonium is broken down into nitrites. The ammonium resulting from decomposition returns to the nitrites—nitrates—protein cycle. The nitrites are converted into nitrates by soil bacteria. Some of the nitrates are degraded into nitrogen gas in the denitrification process. This gaseous nitrogen is returned to the atmosphere. But at the source of most nitrogen is bacteria on plants, which "fix" the nitrogen into ammonia.

(See more examples in Writing Task 1 from Sample Test Two in Part One and Sample Test Six in Part Five.)

Exercise 4

1. Write a short passage to describe the life-cycle of schistosome.
   (A sample writing is provided.)

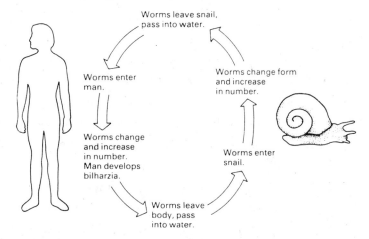

2. Write a short passage to describe a water treatment cycle.

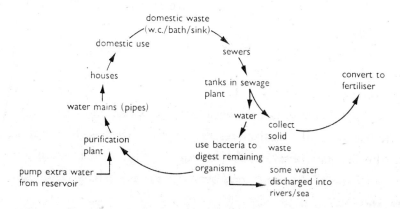

4.3. The Combination of Static and Process Description (静物描述与过程描述的组合)

In academic writing, especially in IELTS, there usually appears the form of a combination of static and process description. The topic is often like this:

"Describe an aerosol container, and explain how it works."

"Describe a tape recorder, and explain how it works."

Read the following example:

Example

Topic: Describe a simple box camera, and explain how it works.

A box camera is simply a box which will let in the correct amount of light for the image to be recorded.

At the front of the camera is a glass lens which projects or throws the image onto a film which is stretched out at the other end of the camera. Just behind the lens is a metal shutter. This can be opened for a very short period of time by pushing a lever called the "shutter release". The shutter will let in only the correct amount of light. The box camera is made so that no other light from any other source can come onto the film. At the top of the camera, there is a piece of glass called the "viewfinder" which is linked to a sort of small glass "window" at the front of the camera on the same side as the lens. This means that by looking through the viewfinder, the photographer can see what picture is going to be taken through the lens. On the same side of the shutter release, there is a film winding knob for winding film on to a fresh piece.

The camera works like this. First a roll of film is loaded in the camera. Then the film is wound on until the number "1" appears in the film window at the back of the camera. Look through the viewfinder and move the camera until what you want to photograph appears clearly. Hold the camera steady and press the shutter release slowly. After a photograph has been taken, the film is wound on by turning the film winder knob until a new number appears. When this has been done, a fresh piece of film is ready to be exposed.

Comment

In the second paragraph, the writer not only describes the position of the important parts of a camera, but also explains the function of those parts. This gives the reader a even better picture of a camera.

Exercise 5

1. Write a short passage to describe a modern camera and explain how it works.
2. Write a short passage to describe a simple walkman and explain how it works.

5. Argument
（议论文）

In IELTS you will have two writing tasks: the first one is often a simple description of an object, a process or some data— something you may have to write as part of a report. The other is often an argument or a discussion on a given topic. In this unit, we will be discussing how to write an argument.

An argument is a set of statements in support of an opinion or proposed course of action. It is expressed in an orderly way, and is used to try to convince someone that the opinion or course of action is correct.

In this unit, we will discuss:

how to plan an argument;

how to support an argument;

how to organize an argument;

how to refute an argument.

5.1. How to Plan an Argument（怎样计划论点）

The first step in planning an argument is to list the points you wish to make. Some of these may be facts. Some may be opinions. Facts are statements which are known to be true. Opinions are personal beliefs which may or may not be true. It is important to distinguish between facts and opinions in arguments. An argument consisting only of opinions will not be convincing to your reader. See the following sentences:

(1) The sun rises in the east.

(2) Jinjiang is a city in Fujian Province.

(3) Jinjiang is a great city.

(4) Styler jeans cost too much.

(5) *The Ghost Show*, which is broadcast on Friday nights, is a terrible programme.

(6) *Book of Nonsense Verse* is Lear's collection of limericks that all children love.

Comment

Sentences (1) and (2) above are facts which can be proved true. Sentences (3) and (4) are personal beliefs which may or may not be true. They need to be proved or supported. Words and phrases like *great* and *too much* are clues that those statements are opinions, not provable facts. Other opinion words are *wonderful*, *ugly*, *boring*, *should*, *must*, etc. Words like these express judgments, for you can not prove that something is "great" or "should" happen. Sentences (5) and (6) are called mixed statements which contain both fact and opinion. The first parts of both sentences above, up through "nights" and "limericks", state facts. The last parts, "is a terrible programme", "that all children love", are opinions. You can find mixed statements in many places, including advertisements, letters to the editor, and editorials. Be sure you understand what is fact and what is opinion in mixed statements.

Exercise 1

1. Which of the following statements are facts and which are opinions? Compare your answers with those of another student and be prepared to justify your choice.
    (1) Smoking cigarettes causes lung cancer.
    (2) Lung cancer is ten times higher among smokers than non-smokers.
    (3) Research indicates that up to 165 people a year are killed by "passive smoking" in Beijing.
    (4) There is no conclusive evidence that "passive smoking" leads to lung cancer. (oret)
    (5) Restrictions on smoking in public places is a threat to individual rights.
    (6) Only weak people smoke cigarettes.
    (7) There is a strong statistical correlation between lung cancer and cigarette smoking.
    (8) Up to 75% of fatal road accidents involve alcohol.
    (9) Drinking alcohol is an anti-social habit.
    (10) People who drink alcohol and then drive are selfish.
    (11) Alcohol drunk to excess impairs judgement of time and distance.
    (12) Drinking alcohol to excess causes brain and liver damage.
2. Read the paragraph. Identify each sentence as a statement of fact or a statement of opinion.

(1) The volume of air traffic at Hart Field has increased 300 percent in the past five years. (2) A recent study shows that the airport's facilities are over-crowded and need repair. (3) It also states that more parking lots are needed. (4) We think a new hotel should be built near the airport. (5) A larger, more modern cargo area would help the city's many factories. (6) Factory owners would prefer to deliver goods by air.

3. Read the paragraph. Identify each sentence as a statement of fact or a statement of opinion, or a mixed statement (mixed fact and opinion).

(1) Every home should have a computer. (2) A computer is a machine that manipulates information in the form of numbers, words, graphics, and pure-ly electronic impulses. (3) Unlike the simple pocket calculator, a computer can be programmed, or instructed, to perform a variety of operations. (4) Home computers are wonderful because they can analyze the performance of your stocks and bonds, monitor your home security system while you are away, and even balance your checkbook. (5) As a word processor, computers are a helpful writing tool, and all school students should have one. (6) Now some computers are so small and light that it is easy to carry them around. (7) It seems likely that, in the future, Chinese households will demand assistance from home computers. (8) Certainly, all school children will have access to one. (9) Within the next ten years, the sale of home computers will probably increase dramatically. (10) New models are coming out every year.

5.2. How to Support an Argument (怎样支持论点)

When you write an argument, you must try to convince your reader that your points are correct. To do so you must provide strong support for your arguments. Here are some ways of supporting an argument:

(1) Supporting an argument by expressing your opinion clearly in a topic sentence.

(2) Supporting an argument by giving relevant and accurate reasons or facts as evidence.

(3) Supporting an argument by giving examples.

(4) Supporting an argument by giving a quotation.

(5) Supporting an argument by mentioning a source.

(6) Supporting an argument by using transition words and phrases that signal your supporting evidence.

5.2.1. Supporting an Argument by Expressing Your Opinion Clearly in a Topic Sentence

A good topic sentence of an argumentative essay should be clear and stick to the point. It can be placed at the beginning or in the middle or at the end of a paragraph. But in IELTS or similar examinations candidates are advised to write the topic sentence at the beginning of a paragraph, because of the time factor. See the following examples:

Example 1

Some doctors think that there is a relationship between automobile accidents and suicide. Many accidents happen because the driver has been drinking. Many others occur because of speed or other reckless driving behaviour. Drivers could avoid all of these factors if they wanted to. Therefore, many doctors suggest that such "accidents" are really self-destructive behaviour on the part of the driver.

Example 2

Professor Birdwhistell believes that physical appearance is often culturally programmed. In other words, we learn our looks — we are not born with them. A baby has generally unformed facial features. A baby, according to Birdwhistell, learns where to set the eyebrows by looking at those around — family and friends. This helps explain why the people of some regions of the United States look so much alike. New Englanders or Southerners have certain common facial characteristics that cannot be explained by genetics. The exact shape of the mouth is not set at birth, it is learned after. In fact, the final mouth shape is not formed until well after permanent teeth are set. For many, this can be well into adolescence. A husband and wife together for a long time often come to look somewhat alike. We learn our looks from those around us.

Comment

The topic sentences of these two examples are both located at the beginning of the passages. The rest of the sentences are developing sentences.

Exercise 2

1. Identify the topic sentence of each paragraph.

87

Paragraph 1

The jury system promotes injustice. Jurors will come to a hasty decision just to shorten the term of service which they find so inconvenient, and so a man may be carelessly acquitted or found guilty, and individual cases will not be given thoughtful consideration. A panel of judges, paid more than adequately by the state, would not be tempted to bring cases to an end: they would have no reason to rush things through, and so each case would be carefully weighed and   a correct verdict reached.

Paragraph 2

Capital punishment is needed for the protection of the community. If an escaping thief knows that if he kills a police officer in pursuit he risks a capital charge, he will hesitate, but if he knows that the penalty will not be substantially different if he is charged with the murder from if he is charged with theft, he will be tempted to kill his pursuer in the hope of escape. Hence capital punishment affords greater security to police officers.

Paragraph 3

Capital punishment is a procedure unworthy of any civilized nation. Even if I were convinced that the abolition of capital punishment would be followed by more murders and crimes of violence, I should still advocate its abolition as human life is sacred and it is absolutely wrong for any community to use the legal killing of human beings as a punishment for crime. "Thou shalt not kill" is the Sixth Commandment and so for Christians and Jews there can be no doubt as to what attitude they should adopt the Scriptures to feel that capital punishment is wrong: everyone will agree that the right to life is a fundamental human right, a natural law which we should not violate.

Paragraph 4

School athletes should participate in school sports but should not be excused from taking a full schedule of other subjects. Athletes should not base all their hopes on having sports careers. Dr. Brown, the famous basketball star, pointed out that all school athletes should prepare for an alternative career, because sports life is usually not long and mostly, only a small number of these athletes might succeed in this career. If students take part in the whole school programme they will be better prepared for life. Much evidence shows that a well-rounded student makes a better and more confident athlete.

2. Read the topics listed below. Write a topic sentence that expresses your opinion for each. (Topic sentences will vary.)
    (1) Working for 44 hours a week
    (2) Studying a foreign language
    (3) Using a computer
    (4) Having a big breakfast
    (5) Taking a walk after supper
    (6) Bicycle parking
    (7) Dogs as pets
    (8) School sports
    (9) Homework
    (10) City recreation centres
    (11) Choosing friends
    (12) Should smoking be made illegal?
    (13) Is money really the root of all evil?
    (14) Divorce
    (15) Advertisement
    (16) Nuclear energy
    (17) Pollution
    (18) An ideal family life
    (19) Public health care
    (20) Retirement

5.2.2. Supporting an Argument by Giving Relevant and Accurate Reasons or Facts as Evidence

An argumentative writing contains statements of reasons or facts and statements of opinions. Knowing what the reasons or facts and opinions are is not enough for supporting an argument. We should give relevant and accurate reasons or facts as evidence. And these reasons or facts can be proved true. See the following example:

Example

Drinking and driving don't mix.

Up to 75% of fatal road accidents involve alcohol.

People drink much more when they are worried.

Comment

The first statement of fact can be proved true. In order to convince the reader that your points are correct, you must provide strong support for your arguments. The second statement is a relevant fact. It supports the argument fairly well. The last statement is a fact but it is irrelevant to this argument.

Exercise 3

Write two relevant supporting statements for each or the sentences below. (Answers will vary.)

(1) Compact cars often cost less than large cars.

   a.

   b.

(2) Everybody should retire at 50.

   a.

   b.

(3) Scientific progress is the result of attempts to meet people's needs.

   a.

   b.

(4) Public money should be spent on persuading people to give up smoking.

   a.

   b.

(5) Education about diet is the most essential feature of a country's health care programme.

   a.

   b.

(6) Education opens the door to opportunity in working life.

   a.

   b.

(7) Computers are an essential part of modern life.

   a.

   b.

(8) Women work twice as hard as men.

   a.

  b.

 (9) Women work longer for less.

  a.

  b.

 (10) The jury system promotes injustice.

  a.

  b.

5.2.3. Supporting an Argument by Giving Examples

Good examples can help your reader understand your points. See the following examples:

Example 1

  Revolutions which overthrow despotic governments by violent means often end by establishing another kind of despotism. A good example is the French Revolution of 1789, which began as an expression of democratic will, and ended by establishing Napoleon as Emperor of the French.

Example 2

  People say that superstitions are all nonsense, but I think there are some things that you must take notice of. For example, my uncle, who was a test pilot, was killed in a plane crash on Friday the 13th, on a trip which my aunt begged him not to take.

Example 3

  I think corporal punishment in all its forms is morally degrading, It does nothing to reform criminals because statistics show that many of those who have suffered corporal punishment for some offence have later committed further offences.

  When I was a boy at school, one teacher was always caning boys for real or imagined offences. He was a complete sadist. I hated him then and I hate his memory now. That is the sort of thing that corporal punishment does.

Exercise 4

Support the following statements by giving examples. (Possible answers are provided.)

(1) The increase in the number of privately owned vehicles on our roads has produced an urban transport problem of great urgency.

(2) It is often asked which of the two sexes is superior. There is conclusive evidence of the superiority of the male sex in all significant respects.

(3) Owning a home provides a number of benefits.

(4) We learn our looks from those around us. This is perhaps why in a single country there are areas where people smile more than those in other areas.

(5) Other people's tobacco smoke seems to increase the chances of non-smokers getting a wide range of cancers.

5.2.4. Supporting an Argument by Giving Quotations

A quotation may consist of a word, phrase, sentence, paragraph or longer expression from the text of another writer. Quoting an authority on a subject is a way of reinforcing an argument and strenthening a point of view. Quotations also add colour and feeling to writing. But take care not to overwork the technique! It is not necessary to substantiate every assertion you make by bolstering it up with a quotation. Choose quotations selectively and use them sparingly.

Concerning presentation, the general rule is that a quotation should correspond precisely to the original regarding wording, spelling, capitalization and punctuation. Quotations should also read properly, i.e., the syntax of your sentence should be grammatically consistent with the quotation.

Quotations are denoted by the use of a quotation mark " ". It encloses all the words quoted. See the following examples:

Example 1

There is general agreement that "Johnson's invectives against Scotland, in common conversation, were more in pleasantry and sport than real and malignant."

Example 2

Solomon said, "Spare the rod and spoil the child". Children don't

92

change. They are the same now as they were in his time.

Example 3

The main issues about which the two articles are in conflict seems to be whether or not the State is "justified" in the use of capital punishment, yet still claim to be "civilized". A secondary issue is concerned with the purpose of the death penalty primarily as a "deterrent", or as a straightforward "punishment".

Exercise 5

Write a paragraph to support an argument by using the following quotations:
(1) "All work and no play makes Jack a dull boy." (a proverb)
(2) "It is very easy to give up smoking. I've done it dozens of times." (Mark Twain)
(3) "Lectures are an economical way of giving information to a large number of students." (R. R. Jordan)
(4) "School uniforms are an excellent idea." (President)
(5) "Prevention first" (government policy)

5.2.5. Supporting an Argument by Mentioning a Source

Mentioning an authoritative source on a subject without actually quoting from it is another way of reinforcing an argument and strengthening a point of view. See the following examples:

Example 1

Recent references in the *New Scientist* indicate that lung cancer is ten times higher among smokers than non-smokers.

Example 2

According to statistics published recently in China that up to 55 % of fatal road accidents involve alcohol.

Example 3

As Professor Hones points out that in an increasingly technological society, some form of tertiary training is fast becoming essential.

Exercise 6

Complete the following sentences:
(1) According to a recent article in *China Daily* that ...
(2) The results of a recent public opinion poll revealed...
(3) According to statistics published recently in China...
(4) The work of scientists in this country confirms the view that...
(5) Experimental work undertaken in this country suggests that...
(6) Official reports indicate that...
(7) Studies in this field have shown that...
(8) The *New Scientist* recently highlighted the findings that...
(9) An article in the *New Scientist* recently demonstrated this point...
(10) There are regular reports of this in the *People's Daily*...
(11) An example of this given by Prof. Wang, in Beijing University, indicates that...
(12) It is clear from Dr David's observations that he considers...

5.2.6. Supporting an Argument by Using Transition Words and Phrases that Signal Your Supporting Evidence

The transition words and phrases used in an argumentative essay include *to begin with*, *first*, *next*, *finally*, *because*, *since*, *more important*, *furthermore*, *besides*, *in addition*, *also*, *as well as*, *more over*, *therefore*, etc. Now study these statements:

(1) An earlier age of retirement has certain advantages.
   a. More opportunities for jobs for younger people.
   b. Ambitious younger workers would be able to reach the top without a lot of older people blocking the way.

Both a and b support statement (1). b provides additional support to make the argument stronger. We can show this by using a transition word.

Example

One advantage of an earlier age of retirement is that there would be more opportunities for jobs for younger people. Moreover, ambitious younger workers would be able to reach the top without a lot of older people blocking the way.

Now read the following paragraph. Notice the usage of transition words.

It is now widely accepted that excessive consumption of refined sugar is not good for us. *To begin with*, refined sugar lacks nutrients and is, *therefore*, not really a food. *Moreover*, refined sugar tends to be retained by the body in the form of fat. *Furthermore*, although sugar initially gives us more energy, it can also contribute to the condition known as hypoglycemia, or low blood sugar levels, leading to loss of energy. *In addition*, of course, refined sugar is a major contributor to tooth decay.

Exercise 7

1. Complete these sets of statements using a reinforcing idea of your own. Then link the statements in each set with transition words.
   (1) Owning a home provides a number of benefits.
       (a) One does not have to worry too much about noise.
       (b) One can redecorate without worrying about losing the deposit.
   (2) There are benefits of renting a home.
       (a) If a renter wants to move, it is not necessary to find a buyer.
       (b) A renter does not have to provide a large down payment as does a home owner.
   (3) Staying single is better than getting married.
       (a) It gives you the freedom to spend your own money in your own life.
       (b) You have the amount of free time to enjoy in any way you prefer.
   (4) Getting married is better than staying single.
       (a) You do not feel lonely.
       (b) You can have fun with your own children.
   (5) Nuclear energy should be developed.
       (a) It is cheap.
       (b) It is clean because it does not pollute the environment.
2. Complete the following passages by selecting words and phrases from the boxes below:

Passage 1
   There are several advantages of learning to type. _____, typing is

much less fatiguing than writing, especially when you use an electric typewriter. You can typewrite for hours without fatigue, while steadily writing for a time will soon tire your hands. _____, no matter how tired you become, the character of typed letters never changes. _____, script will tend to become sloppy after long periods of writing. _____, typing is always legible with a minimum of effort. At times personal script is so poor that it is difficult, if not impossible, to read. Legibility can contribute to an improved grade, _____ a teacher is more likely to give a low grade to a sloppily written paper than to a neat, typewritten one.

> first, next, on the other hand, second, since

Passage 2

Being fat is not quite as bad as it seems. Cute overweight girls have more to admire when they look into mirrors. When they find a nice dress, there is more of it to look nice in. _____ , it is economical to be corpulent; because it costs the same for a size 16 as it does for a size 10, fat girls certainly get more for their money. _____, a pleasingly plump lassie never has to be afraid of being called "Twiggy". _____, in the case of a great famine as the result of the expanding population, tubby girls will live longer than thinner members of their sex. In old age, overweight girls will never have to find outside hobbies to fill up their time, _____ they will be constantly occupied with grocery shopping and letting out seams in their clothes. _____, fat girls have one last fringe benefit: there is more of them for their boy friends to love. _____, do not count your calories, girls. Let it all hang out!

> besides, finally, for, furthermore, in addition, therefore

5.3. How to Organise an Argument （怎样组织论点）

A good argument has to be effectively organized so that your reader can follow the chain of argument and be convinced by it. In academic writing two methods are quite often used in an argumentative essay. They are called the deductive method （演绎法） and the inductive method （归纳法）. When we use the deductive

96

method, the main statement is made at the beginning followed by a supporting statement or statements. When we use the inductive method it is effective to outline the evidence (supporting statements) first and present the main point last as a conclusion.

Read the following examples:

Example 1

Ask most people what causes strikes and they will probably say: more money! In fact, there are many causes of strikes. Moreover, a single strike could have a number of causes rather than a single cause.

Obviously, the demand for more money is a major cause of strikes. A second cause is the demand for improved working conditions. But "working conditions" covers many things. It includes the physical environment of the workplace, such as the quality of eating and recreational facilities, together with the safety and cleanliness of the workplace itself. "Working conditions" also includes the psychological climate of the workplace.

Quite often when a strike is called the official reason given is inadequate pay. But industrial psychologists have found that this may be disguising the real reasons. Such reasons might be the unpleasant attitude of a supervisor or a company official, or it might be the tedium of highly repetitive work.

Furthermore, the workers themselves may not be aware of these "hidden" reasons. They may only be aware of a general dissatisfaction, and "inadequate pay" may just be a convenient excuse for expressing that dissatisfaction.

In addition to expressing dissatisfaction, strikes have the effect of breaking the monotony of repetitive work.

In conclusion, although demanding for more money is usually the main reason of strikes, there are also some other reasons.

Example 2

Did you realise that at least one third of household garbage is food waste? And did you know that a significant proportion of domestic waste taken to tips is garden refuse?

Most food and garden wastes can easily be turned into compost which will improve the quality of your garden soil. In turn, better soil will produce better flowers, vegetables, lawn, shrubs and trees.

In addition to these benefits, we can reduce air pollution by avoiding burning-off and putting waste materials into a compost heap instead. Just think: you will have happier neighbours (no more complaints about the burning-off), reduced car fuel bills (not as many trips to the tip), and less rubbish for the council to take away. Besides, compost is easy to make and pollution-free.

All of these things add up to a pretty convincing argument in favour of all households having their own compost heap.

Comment

Example 1 uses the deductive method. The structure is like this:

> Introduction: There are many causes of strikes. A single strike could have a number of causes rather than a single cause.
> Supporting statement 1: demand for more money
> Supporting statement 2: demand for better conditions
> Supporting statement 3: breaking the monotony
> Conclusion: Strikes have many causes.

Example 2 uses the inductive method. The structure is like this:

> Introduction: At least one-third of household garbage is food waste. Much domestic waste taken to tips is garden refuse.
> Main point 1: Compost turned from food and garden waste could make better soil.
> Main point 2: Air pollution is reduced.
> Conclusion: All households should have their own compost heap.

Exercise 8

Study these groups of sentences. Identify the main point in each group and then organise the sentences into an effective argument by using either a deductive method or an inductive method. (with suggested answer)

98

(1) a. Nonetheless, in Australia at present, fewer than 6% of the population have a university degree.

    b. On the contrary, most authorities are of the opinion that young people should stay at school for as long as possible.

    c. Without such training, career prospects can be very limited.

    d. These days few people would suggest that children leave school as early as possible.

    e. There are fewer and fewer opportunities for people without the kinds of skills acquired at technical college or university.

    f. In fact, in an increasingly technological society, some form of tertiary training is fast becoming essential.

    g. Besides, to obtain the full benefits of living in a modern urban society, people need a well-rounded education.

    h. This is a disappointing situation, not only for the people who have missed out on higher education, but also for the country as a whole which needs well-educated people.

(2) a. We must never let outsiders use Foothill Park.

    b. Nobody from our city can use these parks anymore.

    c. Look at what has happened to our other parks that outsiders are allowed to use.

    d. It has to be saved for residents.

    e. The outsiders never clean up their trash, and they constantly blast their radios so that they disturb residents who live nearby.

    f. Early every weekend morning, the picnic tables are always taken by outsiders.

    g. I disagree with the article saying we should allow people from surrounding communities to use our city's Foothill Park.

(3) a. Husbands seem to benefit much more from marriage than wives do.

    b. Various explanations have been considered, but the most plausible is that wives provide more social support than husbands.

    c. They are more exposed to stresses at work, and have worse health, and die earlier than women.

    d. Despite the benefits of marriage, women find it stressful, and are in better shape if they also have jobs; their earnings and status increase their power in the home, and they may also get social support at work.

    e. Successful marriage is the most effective form of social support.

    f. It relieves the effects of stress, and leads to better mental and physical health.

g. Married women are in better physical and mental health, and are happier than single women, but these effects are nearly twice as great for men.

h. Perhaps men need it more?

i. In addition, when women get married, their way of life is subject to much greater change and this often leads to boring and isolated work in the home for which they are ill-prepared.

5.4. How to Refute an Argument（怎样反驳论点）

If there were no evidence for an alternative point of view, there would be no need for argument. A good argument always takes the opposing point of view seriously. If this were not the case, the argument would be more like a quarrel, consisting of the exchange of opinions and prejudices without support from evidence or reasoning. When you are writing, your refutation should do one of the following:

re-state the opinion;

correct your opponent's facts;

deny that the counterargument is related to the topic;

indicate that the counterargument is insufficient.

5.4.1. Re-state the Opinion

When you want to refute an argument, you need to re-state the opinion, so the person you are writing to can understand. To show that we do not personally hold the opinions we intend to refute, we often write them as reported speech. Here are some examples:

(1) Some people assert that all pop music is rubbish.

(2) It is ridiculous to say that English should be taught everywhere.

(3) It used to be stated that there were jobs which women were physically incapable of doing.

(4) In his article, H. Brown suggests that the main reason for the rapid increase in oil prices was the cost of the Arab-Israeli wars.

Exercise 9

Complete the following sentences: (Answers may vary.)

(1) Some people believe that...

(2) Some people claim that...
(3) Some people maintain that...
(4) The idea which can not be accepted is that...
(5) Few people are of the opinion that...

5.4.2. Correct Your Opponent's Facts

Correcting your opponent's facts is one way to show that the counterargument is not true.

Example

(*Your opponent's facts*) Some people say that cutting trees harms the environment and destroys valuable natural resources. (*You rcorrection*) Selective harvesting is actually good for forests and for people because it increases productivity and provides jobs and timber.

Exercise 10

Correct the ideas in the following sentences: (Answers may vary.)
(1) Some people say that watching TV stops people thinking for themselves.
(2) A. Smith suggests that whale killing should not be banned for Eskimos.
(3) Some people maintain that all required university courses are boring.
(4) Science fiction books are not worth the time it takes to read them.
(5) Happy families make happy children.

5.4.3. Deny that the Counterargument is Related to the Topic

When the topic is something about "insufficient public transportation" and the writer's purpose is to persuade people to agree with the idea of changing and expanding the bus system, but the writer talks a lot about the nice drivers and free fare for university students, it shows that his argument is not relevant. You can write: "although nice drivers and free fare for students is true, it is not related to the topic."

Exercise 11

Write one paragraph for each of the following to deny that the idea is related to the topic: (Answers may vary.)

(1) Topic: negotiation skills in business administration

Purpose: to persuade the audience about the critical importance of negotiation skills in business administration.

Counterargument: There are only three main negotiation skills in business administration.

(2) Topic: the use of chemical additives in food processing

Purpose: to persuade the audience that the advantages derived from the use of chemical additives in food processing outweigh the disadvantages.

Counterargument: The introduction of different kinds of chemical additives in food processing brings about prosperity.

(3) Topic: the laws which prohibit the sale and consumption of heroin

Purpose: to illustrate that the laws which prohibit the sale and consumption of heroin should not be applied to tobacco.

Counterargument: Smoking tobacco takes less dangers.

5.4.4. Indicate that the Counterargument is Insufficient

When you want to refute an argument, you could compromise that although the counterargument is true, it is not enough to overcome your arguments.

Example

Although instant noodles are fast and quite easy to fix, sitting down to a dinner that tastes like cardboard and is not much nutritious makes eating not very worthwhile.

Exercise 12

Write a statement for each to show that the following ideas are not sufficient: (Answers may vary.)

(1) Cutting trees causes erosion and landslides, and destroys natural resources.

(2) Cars are very convenient. It can be fairly quick to send you to anywhere you want to go.

(3) Solar energy systems are initially costly and presently have relatively low efficiency.

(4) Vegetables grow faster and bigger with chemical fertilizers.

(5) Plastic products are light and cheap.

6. Report
(报告)

In IELTS the candidates are likely asked to look at a diagram, table, or perhaps a short piece of text and to turn their findings and recommendations into a report. A report should be an orderly and objective communication of facts aimed at a particular reader for a specific purpose. A well-written and effective report must therefore be as accurate, factual, clear and complete as possible in itself and easy to read. A report must be well-organized with one part logically following or explaining another part. A logical structure of a report is usually as follows:

Introduction
    1. Terms of reference (what you have been asked to find out)
    2. Procedure (how you found out the information)
Body
    3. Findings (what you found out)
Conclusion
    4. Conclusions (your conclusions, or diagnosis)
    5. Recommendations (what you think should be done)

These five points form the structure of any report regardless of its length. Now let's look at a short report:

I have checked all the computers in our computer centre yesterday. Most of the computers were working all right but some have already caught virus. I think these computers should not be used before removing the virus. A virus check-up card should be stored in every computer.

Comment

This is a good report. It is useful and short and gives clear, well structured information. The report contains the terms of reference (the state of the computers), the procedure (a personal check), the findings (most computers are all right but some are wrong), the conclusions (those computers should not be used before removing the virus), and the recommendation (a virus check-up card should be stored in every computer).

Now let's look at some sample tasks from IELTS.

Sample task 1

The diagram below illustrates some of the processes in the production of coloured paper-clips at a small factory. As a member of the Quality Circle, you have been asked to comment on the process and to consider whether any changes are necessary.

Task: For the first part of your report, you must describe the current process of producing plastic paper-clips. Use the diagram below to help you describe the process.

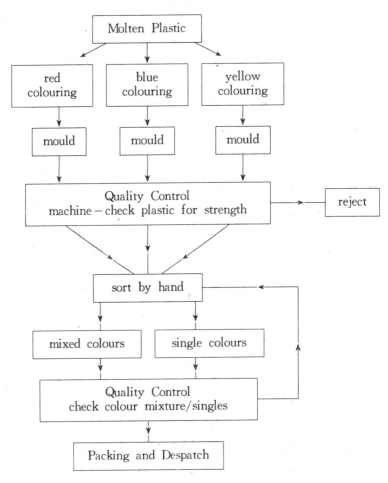

Sample task 2

You have been asked to write a report for a scholarship committee on the adjustments that overseas students need to make.

Task: Describe the most important adjustments to learning and writing styles you feel overseas students are likely to need to make and give advice on how they should do this.

Sample task 3

Scientists generally agree that the world is facing the prospect of substantial global warming unless countermeasures are taken immediately.

Task: As a university assignment, write a report on the likely effects of global warming on the capital city of your country. Include what you consider to be the priority recommendations to counter these effects.

Sample task 4

Task: Write a short report outlining the main findings of a national opinion survey on the British educational system. The results are shown in the questionnaire below. (Some parts are omitted.)
         C: children   T: teachers   P: parents

The Aims of Education
    Question: What do you think the main aim of children's education should be? Is it:

	C	T	P
to prepare them for everyday life?	20%	39%	32%
to help them develop their true selves?	73%	3%	48%
None of these	0%	2%	0%
Don't know	1%	14%	1%

Standard of Education

Question: Overall, how do you rate the standard of secondary education in schools?

	Excellent	Good	Average	Poor	Don't know
C:	13%	53%	32%	1%	1%
T:	28%	61%	8%	1%	2%
P:	17%	46%	28%	8%	1%

Obviously, all these four samples are report writing tasks. Sample 1 requires the writer to be a member of the Quality Circle to write a report which contains two elements. One is to write a description of the current process of producing plastic paper-clips based on the diagram given. The other is to provide some comments on the process.

Sample 2 is more or less the same as sample 1. Of the two elements one is to write a description on the most important adjustments to learning and writing styles the writer feels overseas students are likely to need to make. The other is to give advice on how they should do this.

Both sample 1 and sample 2 are forms of writing task 1 of IELTS. Although sample 3 is a form of task 2 in IELTS, it is basically the same as the samples 1 and 2. We can call this kind of report a how-to report with comments or recommendations. A how-to report explains how to do or make something according to a step-by-step process.

Sample 4 is a report based on statistics. The function of a report of this kind is to organize the facts so that the most important findings become clear to the reader. The function is not to systematically reproduce every detail of the statistics since the diagram does that in a more accessible way.

In this unit we will deal with these two kinds of reports. Before you write a report, you should know clearly who your audience will be —a Quality Circle, a scholarship committee, a university teacher, a friend who already knows something about your topic, a person who is unfamiliar with it, or someone who has a particular interest in it. Make sure you have a clear idea of your purpose. This will help you keep to the point so that your directions are as clear as possible.

6.1. Writing a How-to Report (写一个怎样做某事的报告)

A well-written how-to report should be:

(1) Clear. The language used must be easily understood by the reader. If the reader knows about the subject of the report, the writer can use technical language;

but if the reader is unfamiliar with the terminology of the subject, then the writer must use simpler language that is easily understood by the non-specialist.

(2) Easy to read. A report must be well-organized with one part logically following or explaining another part, so the reader can grasp the meaning quickly. This can be done by using transition words and phrases to connect the steps.

Example 1

Process of Producing Plastic Paper-clips

As a member of the Quality Circle, I have examined the current process of producing plastic paper-clips.

The steps of production are as follows:

First, molten plastic is transferred into three different coloured tanks — red, blue and yellow. Then, each of them is led to a mould. After moulding, the three kinds of coloured paper-clips are put together in the quality control section, there they get a machine check for strength. If the product is not up to standard, it will be rejected at this step. Those qualified products will be sorted by hand into two parts. One is for mixed colours, and the other for single colours. Then both will go to the second quality control section which is for checking colour mixture and singles. If some products are not up to the standard, they will be put back to the sorting section. Finally, those well-made products will be then moved to the packing and despatch section.

Generally speaking, the whole process is very well designed, but the sorting section needs to be improved. In a large-scale production, if all the products are sorted by hand it will either slow down the production speed or more labours need to be hired. It is suggested that the first quality control section is divided into three parts, following directly from the moulding section. After the checking, according to the percentage required coloured products either go into the colour mixture section or the single colour section. This is the only place which needs to be changed.

Example 2

The Right Machine for the Job

V.S.O. is a world aid organisation with a great deal of experience in developmental strategies, as applied to the "Third World". Their promotional literature is designed to aim at the heart of the problem and the experience of its readers. It describes the attempts of successive experts to upgrade the technology level of an African village.

In the first stage, the process begins with what is seen as the problem. Hoes and spades are used by the women to cultivate the fields.

A tractor is provided for them by the first expert. Interest is maintained, and gender-roles are reversed for three weeks, until the breakdown of the tractor. The difficulty of obtaining spare parts ensures that the new technology is discarded, as the people have neither the skills nor materials to maintain it. The older, more reliable technology is re-instated.

The second stage is marked by the arrival of Expert Number Two, who is able to offer more practical help than the first. This also represents the shift which occurred in Aid Agencies' thinking at that time. A flour-mill is provided, powered by bicycle. It is equally unsuccessful, because it fails to either motivate the men, or to take account of the social and cultural customs of the village.

The final stage of the process describes how a third expert, presumably reflecting the current Developmental Agency policies, does not seek to impose a solution from the outside. The villagers are asked instead to analyse their own problems, and then to suggest possible practical solutions. At this point, the injection of a relatively small amount of cash from the Development organization enables the purchase of better quality tools and the upgrading of the skills of the smith.

This innovation is more likely to be successful and sustainable, as ownership of the change belongs to the village, and the technology can be both maintained and transmitted.

Exercise 1

1. As a university assignment, write a report on the likely advantages and disadvantages of studying abroad.
2. Write a report on the listening challenges the overseas students may face. Provide recommendations you would offer.
3. Write a report on the likely causes of the erosion of the land. Include what you consider to be the priority recommendations to solve the problem.

6.2. Writing a Report Based on Statistics (写一个有关统计数字的报告)

When you write a report based on statistics you should always remember that the function of a report of this kind is to organize the facts so that the most important findings become clear to the reader. The function is not to systematically reproduce every detail of the statistics since the diagram does that in a more accessible way.

Example

The following table shows the percentage of the Earth's surface area and the percentage of the world's population for the seven continents.

Task: Write a short report outlining the main findings of the area and polulation of the continents.

Area and Population of the Continents

Continents	Area	Population
Asia	30%	58%
Africa	20%	11%
North America	16%	9%
South America	12%	5%
Antarctica	9%	0%
Europe	7%	16%
Oceania	6%	1%

Sample writing:

According to the statistics shown in the table, the continent which occupies the largest land area in the world is Asia. Asia is also the most populated continent—over half of the world's population lives here. Asia is obviously much more densely populated than Africa. Even though the two continents are about the same in physical size, the population of Asia is five times greater than that of Africa.

However, Asia is not yet the most densely populated continent. Europe, with the second highest population and the second smallest land area, is the most densely populated continent. The least populated continent is Antarctica. While it has a land mass larger than Europe or Oceania, virtually no one lives there.

North America is more than twice as large as Europe, but has only slightly more than half of the population of Europe. With the exception of Antarctica, Oceania has the smallest population. South America has twice the physical area of Oceania and five times more people.

Even though the physical area of North and South America combined is nearly the same as that of Asia, Asia has more than three times their combined population. Asia has slightly less physical area than the combined areas of Africa and South America, but still has more than double their population.

Exercise 2

1. Write a short report that conveys the following information:

Vehicles Crossing the Waterloo Bridge

Time	Passenger Car	Lorry
Sunday	2000	500
Monday	2000	1500
Tuesday	1500	2000
Wednesday	1500	1000
Thursday	1500	1500
Friday	2000	1000
Saturday	1500	500

2. The following table gives information about family spending in China. Look at the information and then write a report with generalized comments that draw attention to the most significant items.

Average Monthly Expenditure Per Family in China

Subjects	Percentage
Food	40 %
Tobacco	5 %
Alcoholic drink	5 %
Fuel, light and water	2 %
Durable household goods	6 %
Transport	15 %
Housing	2 %
Clothing and footwear	15 %
Other goods	10 %

3. Over the last 20 years women have joined the paid work force in ever increasing numbers. Write a short report outlining the main findings of the following diagram with necessary comments.

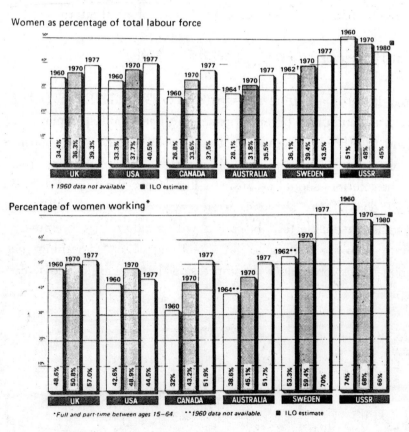

111

7. Letter Writing
（信件写作）

Letters can be grouped as being formal or informal. Formal letters can be either formal impersonal or formal personal. For example, a letter to the principal of a college explaining why you will be delayed is a formal impersonal letter. A letter to the father of a friend of yours thanking him for a holiday arrangement is a formal personal letter. A letter to a friend of your own age congratulating him or her on an examination success will probably be written as an informal letter (a personal letter). When you write a letter, you'd better always remember that the worst mistakes in letter writing are caused by mixing up the different kinds. Different occasions require different treatment. The kind of letter that works in one situation won't be any good in others. In this unit we will discuss the techniques used in writing formal impersonal, formal personal and informal letters.

7.1. Formal Impersonal Letters （正式非私人信件）

Formal impersonal letters are written TO GET THINGS DONE. They are written to firms and other organizations, to offices and departments, to employers of firms and to officials. Because of this they are often called "business letters". For this reason, the rules of formal impersonal letter writing must be strictly obeyed. These letters should be business-like. Concentrate on the business you are trying to get done. Don't bury it in irrelevant personal details. When you are writing a formal impersonal letter, be careful with handwriting, grammar, punctuation and spelling. You are writing to get something done, something that matters to you. So don't give your reader the impression that you are careless. See the following example:

Example

(1) Registry
Old College
South Bridge
Edinburgh EH8 9YL
30th October, 1996

(2) Mr. J. Smith
Director of the English Section
Kenneth Machenzie House
27 Lauder Road
Edinburgh EH9 2JG

(3) Dear Mr. Smith:

(4) I am writing to let you know that we are holding in the Registry your Latin parchment which has been returned from the calligrapher. Please send by return of post old certificate and your cheque for 20 pounds (made out to the University of Edinburgh). I look forward to hearing from you.

(5) Yours sincerely,

(signature)

(6) J. Harrison
Senior Administrative Officer
Registry

This is a typical formal impersonal letter (business letter). This kind of letter should be typewritten except the signature. It consists of six parts:

(1) Heading. The return address goes in the top right-hand corner of the page with the date below it. Do not put your name above or near your address. Remember always to use the postcode. (e.g. EH8 9YL)

(2) Inside Address. Write the name of the receiver and the inside address on the left and four to six lines below the return address.

(3) Salutation. Write the salutation on the left, two lines below the inside address, and follow it with a colon (:). The normal ways of naming the person you are writing to are as follows:

a. If you know the name of the person, you write:

Dear + Mr/Mrs/Ms/Miss + surname

b. If you don't know the name of the person, you write:

Dear + Sir or Madam/Sir (s)

(4) Body. Start your letter on the left-hand side, underneath the name two lines below.

(5) Closing. Write the closing on the left-hand side, and follow it with a comma (,). When you know the name of the person you are writing to, use the form: Yours sincerely. If you don't know the name of the person you are writing to, it is usual to use the form : Yours faithfully.

(6) Signature. You should write your signature three or four lines down below the closing by hand. Below your signature you should print or type your name, so that the person who reads your letter is in no doubt about who you are.

Exercise 1

1. Write to the Student Accommodation Office telling them what your situation is, what accommodation you wish to have and ask for any suggestions. Use your own real return address.

Inside Address: Student Accommodation Office
30 Buccleuch Place,
Edinburgh EH8 9JS

2. Write to the secretary of the Department of Applied Linguistics, University of Edinburgh, explaining why you will be delayed, expressing your concern about missing first week's classes, and asking what you should do.

Inside Address: Mrs J. Smith
Department of Applied Linguistics,
University of Edinburgh,
14 Buccleuch Place
Edinburgh EH8 9LN

3. Write to the course supervisor of the Institute for Applied Language Studies, telling her what courses you are applying for and what you think your strong points are.

Inside Address: Ms S. Gellaitry
Institute for Applied Language Studies,
University of Edinburgh,
21 Hill Place, EH8 9DP
Edinburgh

7.2. Formal Personal Letters（正式私人信件）

Formal personal letters are different from formal impersonal letters because the relationship between the writer and the reader is different and the letters are written about different kinds of things. The writer of a formal personal letter knows the reader personally. The purpose of the letter is to send a message from one person to another person. You are not writing about a "business" or an "official" subject. The way you write the letter must show your reader that you are thinking of him or her in a personal way.

Formal personal letters are formal, so, your letters should be properly set out and carefully written. This kind of letter often covers the following areas：

   a. invitation
   b. requests
   c. arrangements
   d. apology
   e. congratulations
   f. thanks

Now see the following example：

Example

(1) Flat 3, Hartington House,
9 Hope Park Terrace
Edinburgh EH8 9JX
9 July, 1996

(2) Dear Mr and Mrs Seaton,

(3)   Thank you very much for taking me with you on that splendid outing to London. It was the first time that I had seen the Tower or any of the other famous sights. If I'd gone alone, I couldn't have seen nearly as much, because I wouldn't have known my way about.

I think the river trip was the best thing of all. London really came alive for me as we saw it from the Thames during that wonderful journey down to Greenwich. It was all tremendously exciting — a day that I shall never forget.

115

Thank you for giving me such a great birthday treat.

(4) Yours sincerely,
(signature)

A formal personal letter could be either typewritten (except the signature) or written by hand. It usually consists of five parts. (Inside address does not appear in a formal personal letter.)

(1) Heading. Your address always goes in the top right-hand corner. The date always goes under the address. This can be written as:

Monday, 28th March

March 28th

28/3/96

28.3.96

(2) Salutation. Write the salutation on the left, and follow it with a comma (,). The normal ways of naming the person you are writing to are as follows:

a. Dear Mr/Mrs/Miss/Ms + surname (family name)

b. Dear + Christian name (first name)

(3) Body. Indent four or five spaces at the beginning of every paragraph.

(4) Closing. Write the closing in the centre of the page. The closing is: Yours sincerely, and follow it with a comma (,).

(5) Signature. You should write your signature two or three lines down below the closing by hand.

When you write a formal personal letter, you must choose your words to suit the kind of relationship you have with that person and the kind of subject you are writing about. For example, you wouldn't write to the father of a friend thanking him for a present in the same way that you would write to the dean of your department putting forward your ideas for changes in the course study. You can write formal personal letters to the people:

a. who are older than you.

b. who are in a position of authority.

c. you have not known for a long time.

d. you are acquainted with.

e. you are not related to.

f. you do not have a lot in common with.

Exercise 2

1. A friend who lives abroad will shortly be visiting your university and has asked

you to make arrangements for his stay. Write a letter informing him of what you have done.

2. You are going to be in London for a couple of days. Two British friends of yours live there. Write a letter to invite them out for a meal — at your expense — while you're there.

3. You came back from London after spending some time with a British family. You would like to stay with them again in April. Write a letter to the family, requesting this.

4. You have just been on a week's holiday with a British family. Write and thank them for the holiday.

7.3. Informal Letters（非正式信件）

Informal letters are also called "personal letters". Often you can write informal letters to the people：
   a. who are about the same age as you.
   b. who have the equal social position as you have.
   c. whom you have known for a long time.
   d. who are close friends of yours.
   e. whom you are related with.
   f. who have many things in common with you.

See the following example：

Example

> (1) 139, South Close,
>   London NW3 2RF
>   20 August, 1996

   (2) Dear Pat,

   (3)   I have exciting news to share! My family spent a week with Grandpa Joe in Edinburgh during the Edinburgh festival. We climbed the Arthur's Seat in Holyrood Park and walked along "The Royal Mile" up to the castle. Down the castle is the famous Princes Street, which is the widest and most impressive of the many wide streets. The city is gay with flags and decorations. We are going again in December. Maybe you could come

with us. It would be fun to have my favorite cousin along! What have you been doing? Write back soon.

(4) With love,
(signature)

The usual rules of an informal letter are more or less the same as the formal personal letters.

(1) Heading. You are always required to write your return address. It's annoying to get a letter from someone who assumes that you know his or her address, when you don't. You should always date the letter.

(2) Salutation. The normal way of naming the person you are writing to is as follows:

Dear + Christian name (first name)
(with a comma after it)

(3) Body. You must put a lot of yourself into an informal letter. You must show your understanding of the feelings and interests of your reader.

(4) Closing. The usual closing is Love, With love, Yours, (with a comma after it).

(5) Signature. Sign your Christian name (first name) two lines down below the closing.

Exercise 3

1. You just had a splendid picnic with your family last weekend. Write a letter to a close friend of yours, telling him/her about the picnic and your feelings.

2. You have been away from home studying in another city. Write a letter to your relatives, telling them your feelings about the city and your life there.

3. You have just passed IELTS. Write a letter, telling this news to your family or your close friends.

Part Four: Testing Skills

（第四部分：测试技巧）

Whenever you write an essay in a writing test, the steps are usually as follows: firstly you analyse the task, then you write a plan. Next, according to the plan you've just written, you write the introductory paragraph, the body, and finally the concluding paragraph. When you finish the writing, it is important for you to check your writing. While doing so, see if you can find and correct any spelling or grammatical mistakes. This part is intended to help you build up such writing skills step by step. See the following patterned plan of essay writing:

Analysing the Task
↓
Writing a Plan
↓
Writing an Introduction
↓
Writing the Body
↓
Writing the Conclusion
↓
Checking the Writing

The time distribution for this pattern is suggested as this: about 10% for analysing the task, 20% for writing a plan, 50% for writing an introduction, body and the conclusion, and 20% for checking the writing. If the whole test time is 30 minutes, for example, the time devoted to task analysis should be 3 minutes; the outline planning takes roughly 7 minutes; the introduction, the body and the conclusion should be 15 minutes; and the checking is about 5 minutes.

1. Analysing the Task
(审题)

Whatever you have to write about, you must make sure that your answer is relevant, that it actually does what you are being asked to do. To do this, you must read the task carefully to find out exactly what you have to do. There are words and phrases which direct you as to what you have to do. We can call these words direction words. Before you do the analysing practice, you need to know the exact meaning of these words. The following direction words often appear in the English writing tasks:

assess: Consider all the facts and decide and judge the quality or worth of what you are discussing.

compare: Emphasize similarities.

contrast: Stress differences in things, events, or problems.

criticize or evaluate: In critisizing, express your own judgment — for and against. In evaluating, give the judgment of authorities as well as your own.

define: Be clear, brief and accurate. Give the limits of the definition. Show how the thing you are defining differs from others in its class.

describe: Often this means to tell or recount in sequence or story form. Or it may mean to give a description.

discuss: Examine carefully; give reasons for and against in discussion form.

explain: Make clear what is meant. You may want to give reasons for differences in results or opinions.

justify: Give reasons for conclusions or decisions.

outline: Organize in outline form with main points and subpoints. The main point here is to classify things in brief form.

prove: Give logical reasons or evidence that a thing is true.

relate: Show the connection between two things.

review (state, summarize): These terms mean much the same thing — to give main points, usually omitting details. A review may imply examining a subject critically.

If you want to fully understand what is required by the writing task you must answer four questions:

1. What is the topic?
2. What is the question?
3. Who will be the audience?
4. What are the task requirements?

1.1. What Is the Topic? (题目是什么?)

In the following examples, the topic of each task has been parenthesized.

Examples

Task 1. Write a short paragraph describing (the nitrogen cycle).
Task 2. Should (water fluoridation) be permitted in your country?
Task 3. Describe (an aerosol container), and explain how it works.
Task 4. What are the stages involved in (the production of paper)?
Task 5. Write a brief report on (pollution) in the United Kingdom over the last three years.
Task 6. Write a brief report on (pollution) in your own country over the last three years.

Comment

In task 1, the topic is "the nitrogen cycle". The question is what its cycle is. You need to write a description about the cycle. The topics in tasks 5 and 6 are the same, but task 5 refers to the United Kingdom, whereas task 6 refers to your own country. If you fail to identify the topic clearly, you will write irrelevant material and score poorly.

During the test, when you are analysing the task, you may use your pens or pencils to parenthesize the topic. In this way, the topic will be identified clearly in front of you.

Exercise 1

Bracket the topic words in the following tasks:

(1) What are the arguments used to justify or oppose the capital punishment?

(2) Is having a college education and a degree all that important today? Explain why you think having a college degree is or is not better than not having one.

(3) Explain why the wind blows from the sea to the land during the day.

(4) Describe the components of hot water system and say where they are located in relation to each other.

(5) What are the potential benefits, to both the individual and the community, of continuing education?

(6) Describe how pure water is obtained from polluted domestic and industrial sources.

(7) To what extent does technological development cause more problems than it solves?

(8) What are the disadvantages of scientific research in your particular field?

(9) In what ways has the test of English changed over the last 15 years?

(10) Is the use of animals in scientific laboratory tests justified?

1.2. What Is the Question? (问题是什么?)

Having identified the topic, you must also clearly identify the question. Candidates who fail to identify the question clearly will write irrelevant material and score poorly. See the following examples:

Examples

Task 1. Describe how a television broadcast can be made of a football game.

Task 2. Describe the central heating system shown in the following diagram.

Task 3. Write a brief report on health care in China over the last 10 years.

Task 4. What are the effects of the unrestricted use of private cars in urban areas?

Task 5. To what degree is a knowledge of computers useful in university study?

Comment

Tasks 1, 2 and 3 are instructions rather than questions. If you want to make a clear understanding of these tasks, you need to translate instructions into questions. See the following:

Task 1. Describe how a television broadcast can be made of a football game. = How can it be made of a football game ?

Task 2. Describe the central heating system shown in the following diagram. = What is it like ?

Task 3. Write a brief report on health care in China over the last 10 years. = What happened?

Tasks 4 and 5 are already question forms. You can simply underline the part of the question. See the following:

Task 4. <u>What are the effects</u> of the unrestricted use of private cars in urban areas?

Task 5. <u>To what degree is</u> a knowledge of computers <u>useful</u> in university study?

Some questions, such as task 4 "What are the effects...?" can be answered with a series of facts. Other questions, such as tast 5 "To what degree is.. . .useful...?" require an answer expressed in terms of degree. These kinds of questions can not be answered with "yes" or "no". In order to make a clear understanding of these questions, it is useful to "translate" them into questions which can be give a "yes" or "no" answer. See the following:

To what degree is a knowledge of computers useful in university study? = Is a knowledge of computers useful in university study?

Exercise 2

Underline or write out the questions in the following tasks:
(1) What are the stages involved in letter sorting?
(2) Is a knowledge of statistics necessary for students in their first year university education?
(3) In your opinion should water fluoridation be permitted in your country?
(4) Would the effort spent on digging the historical relics have been better spent on projects of more direct benefit to mankind?
(5) What advice would you offer to a student with reading difficulties?

(6) To what extent has the diet of the Chinese people changed over the past 15 years?

(7) In what circumstance can birth control be justified?

(8) Describe the most important adjustments to learning and writing styles you feel overseas students are likely to need to make.

(9) Write a description of the process of refuse sorting and the equipment needed for carrying it out.

(10) Describe the effects of smoking and methods of risk reduction.

1.3. Who Will Be the Audience? (谁将是读者?)

In academic writing, and in IELTS as well, the audience will generally be a university teacher, an agency such as a sponsoring authority or a university administration. The writing tasks or the requirements will tell you the audience you are writing for. See the following examples:

Example 1

Task: As a course assignment you are asked to write a description of how urban refuse is sorted for recycling. Using the information in the diagram, write a description of this process and the equipment needed for carrying it out.

Example 2

Task: Write an essay for a university teacher on the following topic: Would the effort spent on raising the Mary Rose have been better spent on projects of more direct benefit to mankind?

Example 3

Task: As a member of the Quality Circle you have been asked to comment on the process of producing plastic paper-clips and to consider whether any changes are necessary.

Comment

The audience of example 1 is obviously the course teacher, because the writing is a course assignment. The audience of example 2 is a university teacher. The teacher requires his students to write an essay, and the students do it for the requirement. The audience of example 3 might be the Quality Circle or some other institutions.

Exercise 3

Find out the audience of the following tasks:

(1) Task: Write a report for your sponsoring agency describing the English language skills overseas students are required of. Make any recommendations you feel are necessary.

(2) Task: As a course assignment you are asked to write a brief paper discussing the advantages and disadvantages of studying abroad.

(3) Task: Write an essay for a university teacher on the following topic: What are the benefits and risks associated with the use of air-conditioning in hospitals? Make any recommendations you feel necessary.

1.4. What Are the Task Requirements? (作文要求是什么?)

Everything written in the writing section might be the task requirements except the topic and question. See the following example:

Example

WRITING TASK 1

You should spend no more than 15 minutes on this task.

You have been asked to write a report for a sholarship committee on the adjustments that overseas students need to make.

Task: *Describe the most important adjustments to language learning styles you feel overseas students are likely to need to make and give advice on how they should do this.*

You may make use of your own knowledge and experience.

Make sure your description is:
1. relevant to the question, and
2. well organized.

You should write at least 100 words.

WRITING TASK 2

You should spend no more than 30 minutes on this task.

Task: *Write an essay for a university teacher on the following topic*:

To what extent does technological development cause more problems than it solves?

In writing your essay, make sure that:
1. the essay is well organized,
2. your point of view is clearly expressed, and
3. your argument is supported by relevant evidence.

You should write at least 150 words.

Comment

Based on these two tasks, we can see that the basic task requirements are as follows:
1. Time allowance. No more than 15 minutes on task 1, 30 minutes on task 2.
2. Task type. Task 1 is a report writing. Task 2 is a university essay.
3. Information sources. Information sources are your own knowledge and experience.
4. Writing techniques. The essay must be well organized. Your point of view must be clearly expressed. The writing must be relevant to the question (task 1). Your argument is supported by relevant evidence (task 2).
5. Produce the required minimum number of words (100 words for task 1, 150 words for task 2).

Exercise 4

Analyse the following writing tasks within 2 or 3 minutes for each. Remember the four steps of analysing a task: find out the topic, understand the question, identify the audience, and know the task requirements.

(1) You should spend no more than 15 minutes on this task.

> *The diagram below illustrates why the wind blows from the sea to the land during the day.*

Task: *As a class assignment you have been asked to do the following task: Write a brief description explaining why the wind blows from the sea to the land.*

You may use your own knowledge and experience in addition to the diagram.

Make sure your description is:
1. relevant to the question, and
2. well organized.

You should write at least **100** words.

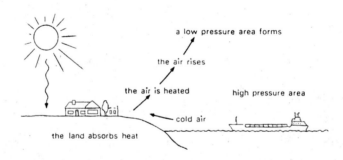

(2) You should spend no more than 15 minutes on this question.

> *The dangers of cigarette smoking are now widely recognised. The diagram below illustrates the effects of smoking and outlines possible measures to reduce the risks involved.*

Task: *As a class assignment your tutor has asked you to write about cigarette smoking. Using the diagram below, write three or four paragraphs describing the effects of smoking and methods of risk reduction.*

You may use your own knowledge and experience in addition to the information provided.

Make sure your description is:
  1. relevant to the question, and
  2. well organized.

You should write at least 100 words.

SMOKING

EFFECTS: reduced fitness; increased risk of heart disease; respiratory diseases

RECOMMENDED METHODS FOR GIVING UP SMOKING: seek advice from a doctor; consult an acupuncturist; attend smokers´ support group

ADVICE FOR SMOKERS: reduce consumption; change to milder brand; use a filter; inhale less smoke

(3) You should spend no more than 30 minutes on this question.

Task: *You have been asked to write a report for a university teacher on the following topic: the use of computers in language teaching activities.*

You should make use of your own knowledge and experience.

In writing your report, make sure that:
  1. the report is well organized,
  2. your point of view is clearly expressed, and
  3. your argument is supported by relevant evidence.

You should write at least 150 words.

(4) You should spend no more than 30 minutes on this question.

Task: *You have been asked to write an essay for a course teacher on the following topic: Is the use of animals in scientific laboratory tests justified?*

You may make use of your own knowledge and experience.

In writing your essay, make sure that:
    1. the essay is well organized,
    2. your point of view is clearly expressed, and
    3. your argument is supported by relevant evidence.

You should write at least **150** words.

2. Writing an Outline
（写提纲）

Most of the writing tests require the candidates to write an essay within the limited time given. In order to organize the thoughts quickly, the candidates should use an outline planning method to organize his thoughts before he begins to write. An essay that is not properly planned will not be organized sufficiently to receive a good score.

When you have analysed the task, you should not write the essay right away, instead, you should gather the useful information or facts to write an outline. Lack of planning can lead to various problems. Running out of ideas when you are only half way through is a common one.

There are various methods of planning, and you should use the method which you are already familiar with. You are suggested to write your outline in English. In this way, you may save your time since you don't need to translate your own language into English when you actually begin your writing.

The most common method of writing an outline is called the standard outline. See the following pattern:

Topic of the essay
Introduction
Paragraph 1 (main point one)
Paragraph 2 (main point two)
Paragraph 3 (main point three)
.
.
.

Conclusion

Since task 1 and task 2 are two different tasks (In task 1 the candidate is often asked to write a description of information given in a diagram. In task 2 the candidate is often asked to write a clear argument or a discussion on a given topic.), the outline writing should be different. In a 15-minute task this should take about two minutes and in a 30-minute task about four or five minutes.

131

2.1. Writing an Outline for Task 1（写作文一的提纲）

Within two minutes, you should:

(1) write the topic at the top of the outline. This will help to focus on your planning.

(2) write the word "introduction", or "intro". This will help remind you to write the introduction.

(3) use your analysis of the question to provide the key ideas that will form the basis of your answer.

(4) write the word "conclusion", or "con". This will help remind you to write the conclusion.

Example 1

What are the stages involved in the letter sorting?

OUTLINE
The Letter Sorting

introduction
stage 1
stage 2
stage 3
stage ?
conclusion

Comment

In this example the key ideas are stages in a process. In other essay outlines they might be some steps, reasons, causes and effects, advantages and disadvantages. Before you collect your information, you do not know how many you will find. So it is useful to keep your outline open by writing a question mark. See some more examples:

Example 2

What are the effects of the unrestricted use of private cars in urban areas?

OUTLINE

The Unrestricted Use of Private Cars in Urban Areas

introduction
effect 1
effect 2
effect 3
effect ?
conclusion

Example 3

Describe an automatic electric oven, and explain how it works.

OUTLINE
Automatic Electric Oven

introduction
part 1
part 2
part 3
part ?
working
step 1
step 2
step 3
step ?
conclusion

Exercise 1

Write an outline for each of the following topics:
(1) What are the likely effects of global warming on the capital city of your country?
(2) Write an essay to describe the steps involved in the process of turning grapes into a drinkable wine.

(3) What are the stages involved in a television broadcast made of a football game?

(4) What are the advantages and disadvantages of studying abroad?

(5) Write a report describing the benefits and risks associated with the use of air-conditioning in hospitals. Make any recommendations you feel are necessary.

(6) Write a report for your sponsoring agency describing the English language skills overseas students are required of. Make any recommendations you feel are necessary.

(7) Write three or four paragraphs to describe a patterned plan of essay writing.

(8) Describe a camera and explain how it works.

(9) Write a short essay describing the life-cycle of a mosquito.

(10) What are the factors which are related to academic success in university students?

2.2. Writing an Outline for Task 2 (写作文二的提纲)

For task 2 of IELTS you will often be asked to write a clear argument or a discussion on a given topic. The topics are usually related to the reading passages. You have to take information from different sources, such as your own knowledge and experience. You have 30 minutes and have to write a minimum of 150 words. The essay has to be presented clearly and logically. Because of this a good outline is even more important for task 2. When you organize your thoughts, you should:

1. write the topic at the top of the outline.
2. write down the topic sentence or phrase of each paragraph.
3. provide some relevant information to support the topic sentence.
4. write down a clear conclusion.

Example 1

As a class assignment you have been asked to write an essay explaining why you should stay single.

OUTLINE
Better to Stay Single

Introduction: Many people believe that staying single is better than getting married.

Why is it so popular?

1. Financial freedom — you can spend your money in any way. What do single people do with their money? Compare with expensive married life — babies, houses, etc.

2. Freedom of time — you can do what you want at any time. You can choose what you want to do, when, where, and with whom you want to do it.

Conclusion: If you want to travel, have a good time, and spend money on yourself, it's best to stay single.

Example 2

Write an essay to describe one or two benefits of owning a home and one or two benefits of renting. Compare the two options and explain which you think might be better for someone your age and in your situation.

OUTLINE
Benefits of Owning and Renting a Home

Introduction: There are both benefits of owning and renting a home. But renting is generally the best choice for young foreign students.

1. Benefits of owning

   It's mine and I can do what I want.

   Do not have to worry too much about noise.

   I can decorate the house with my own will.

2. Benefits of renting

   Not tied down to it.

   Free to move whenever possible.

   Do not have to worry about repairing expenses.

Conclusion: Renting is better for foreign students.

   Not tied down to it.

May transfer to another school.

Will return to own country after school.

Comment

Often, when we discuss something, there are things to be said in favour of it and things to be said against it. So, before we reach a decision and express our opinion, we try to weigh up the *fors* and *againsts*.

Before beginning to write them, draw up a list of the advantages and disadvantages and try to classify them into some sort of order.

Example 3

Some people think that everyone should retire at 50. *What are the advantages and what are the disadvantages? What is your view?*

OUTLINE
Advantages and Disadvantages of Retirement at 50

Introduction: There are both advantages and disadvantages.
1. advantages
    More jobs for the public
    Faster promotion
    Time to do what one wants to while still healthy
2. disadvantages
    Loss of experienced people
    Cost of pensions
    People don't know how to use leisure
    Some people enjoy working
Conclusion: The idea that everyone should retire at 50 possesses more disadvantages than advantages.

Exercise 2

Write an outline for each of the following topics:
(1) Write a report describing the advantages and disadvantages of using computers in your particular field. Make any recommendations you feel are necessary.

(2) As a class assignment you have been asked to write an essay explaining why you should get married.

(3) Assess the contribution made to the quality of life by advances in science and technology.

(4) "Achievement in science is due to an equal blend of revelation, creation, modification and enhancement." To what extent do you agree with this view?

(5) "Man learns from his mistakes." To what extent do you agree with this assertion?

(6) According to some medical experts, nutrition is a more critical factor affecting a nation's health than any of the medical advances of the last two centuries. To what extent do you agree with this concept?

(7) What do you think should be the main components of a preventive medical care programme in a developing country?

(8) In what ways are past improvements in people's living conditions responsible for global or local environmental damage? What can be done to remedy the problems?

(9) What are the outcomes of education? Are exams good selectors?

(10) Give an account of the major problems faced by non-native speakers studying overseas in Western universities. Make any recommendations you feel are necessary.

3. Writing an Introduction
(写导语)

After analysing the task and writing the plan the next step is to write. It is suggested that you spend several minutes here to think carefully about what you are going to say before writing. Because if you make a good start, it will be easier for you to keep your thoughts around the key elements of the topic smoothly through to the end.

There are many ways to write an introduction, and none of them are "wrong". However, this unit will suggest methods of writing introductions for descriptive and argumentative essays, as well as reports.

3.1. Writing an Introduction for a Descriptive Essay (写描述文导语)

The purpose of the introduction is to introduce the topic to your audience and make him clear about what you are going to write. In this section we shall be looking at how to write an introduction for a descriptive essay that describes a process, an object or a set of data (which may be a graph, a chart or a set of figures in a table).

3.1.1. Writing an Introduction for an Essay Describing a Process

With a process you must describe HOW something works or how it is used. For this you should:

1. focus on a series of steps, stages or procedure in processes,
2. tell the audience the numbers of steps or stages,
3. not give much details here, (They should be displayed in the body part of the essay.)
4. write one or two sentences. (Because writing task 1 is relatively short.)

See the following examples:

Example 1

Topic: Describe the process of sorting letters.

138

Introduction: Sorting letters is not a very complicated process although there are eight steps of doing the job.

Example 2

Topic: Using the flow diagram as a guide, describe the nitrogen cycle.

Introduction: This flow diagram illustrates the nitrogen cycle which contains ten stages.

Exercise 1

Write introductions for the following topics:
 (1) What are the stages involved in the production of wine?
 (2) Write three or four short paragraphs setting out the steps for copying from hard disk to diskette.
 (3) Write a short paragraph describing the admissions procedure to 2 institutions for overseas students.
 (4) What are the stages involved in the production of paper?
 (5) Describe how pure water is obtained from polluted domestic and industrial sources.
 (6) Describe how a television broadcast can be made of a football game.
 (7) Write a description of the process of refuse sorting and the equipment needed for carrying it out.
 (8) Describe how to make English tea.
 (9) Describe how to mend a flat bicycle tyre.
 (10) Describe how to take a picture.

3.1.2. Writing an Introduction for an Essay Describing an Object

With an object or a set of objects you must describe WHAT something is or what it does. For this you must focus on the relationship between its parts.

Example

Topic: Describe an automatic electric oven.

Introduction: An automatic electric oven mainly consists of four parts.

Exercise 2

Write introductions for the following topics, describe:

(1) a pocket calculator

(2) a car

(3) a camera

(4) a balance

(5) a stopwatch

3.1.3. Writing an Introduction for an Essay Describing a Set of Data

With data you must describe changes, differences or trends. Focus on WHAT these are and WHY. In the introduction, you could just mention the topic of the essay.

Example 1

Topic: Use the information in the graph to write an essay to describe the changes in the popularity of cinema and television between 1957 and 1974.

Introduction: The following graph shows the changes in the popularity of cinema and television between 1957 and 1974.

Example 2

Topic: Study the pie graph and write an essay to describe consumer purchases of durable goods in 1992.

Introduction: The pie graph shows the consumer purchases of durable goods in 1992. The purchases reflect the economic conditions of the period.

Exercise 3

Write introductions for the following topics:

(1) Use the information in the graph to write a description about outdoor activities in some Western European countries in 1988.

(2) Study the chart below and then write a description about the university full-time students: subject groups of study.

(3) Use the information in the table to write a description about these pairs of binoculars.

(4) Look at the table below and write a description about the similarities and

differences of these four colour television sets.

(5) Study the following two graphs and then write an essay to describe the average family expenses in 1989.

3.2. Writing an Introduction for an Argumentative Essay (写议论文导语)

The introduction for an argumentative essay is different from that of a descriptive essay. An argumentative essay is usually a discussion of a topic, giving reasons why the writer holds a particular point of view. Most academic papers or articles are laid out in such a way that the introduction sets out the problem, and the paragraphs that follow give supporting arguments for the writer's point of view.

If you look carefully at most professionally written academic articles, you will find that the introduction is laid out more or less like this:

1. giving necessary background information about the topic,
2. indicating the issue you plan to develop in the body of your essay,
3. concluding with a statement that sets out your own opinion on the topic.

Example 1

Topic: Football Violence
    (1) In the article about the role of the police in the handling of football crowds, the writer suggested that police should be armed with 2-metre clubs with spikes on the end. (2) Is arming the police really the right way to go about solving law and order problems at sports events? (3) There are, actually, more sensible ways of dealing with law and order at sports events.

Example 2

Topic: A Home for Young Foreign Students
    (1) Many find it advantageous to purchase a home, but others find renting more suited to their needs. (2) Which might be better for young foreign students? (3) Although there are advantages for both options, renting is generally a better choice.

Comment

Both examples are quite good introductions. The numbers in the paragraphs refer to the three parts mentioned above. The second part (the issue) is perhaps the most important part of an introduction, because it helps to make clear what the essay is going to be about. Each issue should be in the form of a question. In writing the introduction, do remember not to:

  a. set out all your wares, (This is for the body.) and

  b. be too general and vague either. (This gives the impression you don't know your subject.)

Now let us look at these three parts separately.

3.2.1. Giving Necessary Background Information about the Topic

The general statement with which you begin your introduction should make your audience interested in your topic. An essay that starts by arousing the tutor's interest is likely to gain more marks than one which doesn't. Giving necessary background information about the topic is one good way of getting to the point. Often you will need to write several sentences to describe the topic, but sometimes only one sentence would be enough. See the following examples:

Example 1

  Last month there were over four hundred violations of traffic rules on the road in London.

Example 2

  The problems of air pollution have been widely reported in the world's press.

Example 3

  It has been said in a report that many people are victims of calcuholism, a dependence on the use of calculators, causing a diminished ability to do mathematics on one's own.

  Question: What essay topics do you think each of these examples is introducing?

Exercise 4

  Look at the following topics and write out some background information about

142

these topics.

    (1) foreign language learning

    (2) the role of universities

    (3) advertisement

    (4) television

    (5) telephone

    (6) divorce

    (7) crime

    (8) city life

    (9) country life

    (10) religion and modern world

3.2.2. Indicating the Issue You Plan to Develop in the Body of Your Essay

The issue defines what the essay is going to be about. This is perhaps the most important part in the introduction , because:

1. by reading the question the audience will know from the beginning what the essay is going to be about,

2. putting down the question helps to clarify the writer's own mind, and

3. it helps the writer to stick to one main point in the essay.

See the following examples:

Example 1

Topic: School Leaving Age

    (1) Recently the school leaving age was raised to fifteen years. (2) Is it really the right way to benefit our society? (3) I think all young people should stay at school until they are eighteen years old, not fifteen.

Example 2

Topic: The Economics of Oil Pricing

    (1) In the article on the use of the "oil weapon" in the 1970s, the writer suggests that the main reason for the rapid increase in oil prices was the cost of the Arab-Israeli wars. (2) But was that really the main reason behind the enormous price increases at that time? (3) There are, actually, other far more important reasons behind the price increases.

143

Exercise 5

Look at the list of topics in Exercise 4. You have already written opening sentences for these topics (or some of them). Now write issues for these topics.

3.2.3. Concluding with a Statement that Sets out Your Own Opinion on the Topic

This statement of your own opinion on the topic can be called the main idea statement. This statement will tell the reader what you think about the issue, and it is the answer to the question posed by the issue. Note that you do not offer any reasons why you hold this opinion in the introduction. You will give reasons in the body of your essay. Now let's see some of the previous examples displayed in this unit.

Example 1

Topic: A Home for Young Foreign Students
(1) Many find it advantageous to purchase a home, but others find renting more suited to their needs. (2) Which might be better for young foreign students? (3) Although there are advantages for both options, renting is generally a better choice.

Example 2

Topic: Football Violence
(1) In the article about the role of the police in the handling of football crowds, the writer suggests that police should be armed with 2-metre clubs with spikes on the end. (2) Is arming the police really the right way to go about solving law and order problems at sports events? (3) There are, actually, more sensible ways of dealing with law and order at sports events.

Exercise 6

Look at the list of topics in Exercise 4. Use the opening sentences and issues you have already written, conclude with a statement that sets out your own opinion on the topic.

144

3.3. Writing an Introduction for a Report (写报告导语)

The introduction for a report usually contains the terms of reference (what you have been asked to find out). See the following example:

Example

Task: Write a report for your sponsoring agency describing the English Language skills overseas students are required of.

Introduction: Overseas students whose first language is not English face a number of language-related challenges. They need to have effective listening, speaking, reading and writing strategies.

Exercise 7

Write introductions for the following tasks:
(1) Write a report to your sponsoring agency describing the accommodation problems faced by foreign students in Britain.
(2) Write a report on the likely effects of global warming on the capital city of your country.
(3) Write a report outlining some of the likely advantages and disadvantages of studying abroad.
(4) Write a report describing the benefits and risks associated with the use of air-conditioning in hospitals.
(5) Write a report describing the factors which contribute to air pollution.

4. Writing the Body
（写正文）

The body is the main part of an essay. It should follow the form of your outline with separate paragraphs for each major topic. Each major topic must be developed fully in a single paragraph and all the paragraphs should be related to each other in some way.

Each paragraph contains one topic sentence and several sentences that explain and illustrate the topic sentence.

4.1. Writing the Topic Sentence （写主题句）

The topic sentence tells the main idea of the paragraph. It should be as clear as possible, so simple sentence is often used. The topic sentence is usually put at the beginning of the paragraph. It could also be placed in the middle or at the end of the paragraph, but for the beginners the topic sentence is better to be placed at the beginning.

The common way of writing a topic sentence for each paragraph is to begin with a restatement of your main idea statement from the introduction.

Example 1

Introduction: Sorting letters is not a very complicated process although there are eight steps of doing the job.

Body: Paragraph 1. (Topic sentence) The first step of letter sorting is to collect letters and packets in bags from pillar boxes, post offices and firms, in post office vans. ...

Paragraph 2. (Topic sentence) The second step of letter sorting is to take these letters to the sorting office, where the bags are emptied and the letters separated from the packets. ...

Paragraph 3. (Topic sentence) The third step of letter sorting is ...

Notice that this essay is a description of a process. The steps are closely connected to each other. In this case we often put these steps in one paragraph and use transition words such as *first*, *then*, *next*, etc. in order to avoid repetition.

Example 2

Introduction: There are three reasons why the nation should keep its airline.

Body: Paragraph 1. (Topic sentence) The first reason why the nation should keep its airline is because it is an important item of international prestige. ...

Paragraph 2. (Topic sentence) The second reason why the nation should keep its airline is because ...

Example 3

Introduction: Although most of the Southeast Asian region is involved in aquaculture, three countries are having the most success in attempting to farm fish in Southeast Asia.

Body: Paragraph 1. (Topic sentence) The first country which is having the most success in attempting to farm fish in Southeast Asia is the Philippines. ...

Paragraph 2. (Topic sentence) The second country which is having the most success in attempting to farm fish is Malaysia. ...

Paragraph 3. ...

Notice that each of your paragraph should take one country in turn.

Exercise 1

Write topic sentences of the body paragraphs of your essay according to the following introductions:

(1) This flow diagram illustrates the nitrogen cycle which contains ten stages.

(2) An automatic electric oven mainly consists of four parts.

(3) The following graph shows the changes in the popularity of cinema and

television between 1957 and 1974.

(4) Many find it advantageous to purchase a home, but others find renting more suited to their needs. Which might be better for young foreign students? Although there are advantages for both options, renting is generally a better choice.

(5) Recently the school leaving age was raised to fifteen years. Is it really the right way to benefit our society? I think all young people should stay at school until they are eighteen years old, not fifteen.

(6) In the article on the use of the "oil weapon" in the 1970s, the writer suggests that the main reason for the rapid increase in oil prices was the cost of the Arab-Israeli wars. But was that really the main reason behind the enormous price increases at the time? There are, actually, other far more important reasons behind the price increases.

(7) In the article about the role of the police in the handling of football crowds, the writer suggests that police should be armed with 2-metre clubs with spikes on the end. Is arming the police really the right way to go about solving law and order problems at sports events? There are, actually, more sensible ways of dealing with law and order at sports events.

(8) Overseas students whose first language is not English face a number of language-related challenges. They need to have effective listening, speaking, reading and writing strategies.

(9) Physical activities and intellectual pursuits are the two basic ways in which we spend our leisure time. While most people have interests in both pastime, we also have favourite ways to spend our time off.

(10) The system of trial by jury is commonly regarded as essential to proper judicial procedure: it is part of the heritage of British justice, and the belief is widespread that the verdict of twelve average people selected at random from the community is likely to be a fair one. But I believe this system is unsatisfactory.

4.2. Writing the Sentences that Explain and Illustrate the Topic Sentence (写展开句)

After the topic sentence, the rest of the paragraph will be the explanatory sentences. In order to give weight to your point of view you can explain or develop the ideas contained in the topic sentence by

1. giving relevant, accurate reasons or facts,
2. giving examples,
3. using transition words and phrases.

4.2.1. Giving Relevant and Accurate Reasons or Facts

After the topic sentence, we add some description or explanation to develop the topic by giving some relevant and accurate reasons or facts. When we explain something we often use "because" to introduce the reason behind it. See the following examples:

Example 1

Topic Sentence: English Food Has a Bad Reputation Abroad.

Explanatory sentences: This is most probably because foreigners in England are often obliged to eat in the more "popular" type of restaurant. Here it is necessary to prepare food rapidly in large quantities, and the taste of the food inevitably suffers, though its quality, in terms of nourishment, is quite satisfactory.

Example 2

Topic Sentence: Corporal Punishment Is Necessary.

Explanatory sentences: ... because it accustoms pupils to the hardships of adult life. If adults break the law, they pay the penalty that justice demands, and so in school too if boys break school rules they should be given the correction of corporal punishment. This is an essential part of character training for the world beyond school.

Exercise 2

Give relevant and accurate reasons or facts after the following statement: (with possible answers)

(1) The process of electing someone to Parliament in Australia can be a complex one. This is because ...

(2) Many people believe that staying single is better than getting married. This is most probably because ...

(3) For millions of years, horses survived in the wild. But when the horse was domesticated and kept in captivity, it became completely dependent on people. Because ...

(4) It is difficult to say what is the real centre of London, but many people would choose Piccadilly Circus. This is because ...

(5) Some people would say that an Englishman's home is no longer his castle, that it has become his workshop. This is partly because ...

4.2.2. Giving Examples

Examples are usually used after a topic sentence. A topic sentence is seldom impressive or convincing. It is necessary to give examples to prove it. Usually we say "for example" or "for instance" to indicate that we are using examples to develop a topic.

Example 1

Topic Sentence: Owning a home provides a number of benefits.

Explanatory Sentences: For example, a homeowner can make more noise than someone who lives in an apartment without having to worry that every small noise might disturb the neighbours.

Example 2

Topic Sentence: Paris is a famous world centre of education.

Explanatory Sentences: For instance, it is the headquarters of UNESCO, the United Nations Educational, Scientific and Cultural Organization.

Exercise 3

Give examples to support the following topic sentences:
(with possible answers.)

(1) The question of equal pay for equal work is not as simple as it appears at first glance. For instance, ...

(2) A "typical" British family used to consist of mother, father and two children, but in recent years there have been many changes in family life. Some of these have been caused by new laws. For example, ...

(3) There are many ways in which people all over the world are the same. For

example, . . .

(4) Carbon is a very special material, and there are atoms of it in many things, for instance . . .

(5) There are many different kinds of musical instruments. They are divided into three main classes according to the way they are played. For example, . . .

(6) Air pollution is not only a result of our civilisation, it can also have natural causes. For example, . . .

(7) Heavy consumption of alcohol is a problem in many societies. In Britain, for instance, . . .

(8) Geothermal energy has been exploited for centuries. The Romans, for example, . . .

4.2.3. Using Transition Words and Phrases

After the topic sentence, usually, you need to develop your ideas. You need to make sure that your reader can follow your ideas. In order to do this, each sentence should follow logically from the previous sentences and each paragraph should relate logically to the one before it. You can make sure your reader understands the relationship between the sentences and paragraphs in your essay by using transition words and phrases. The following transition words and phrases are often used in the English writing test:

1. Indicating Time Relationships

   (They are appropriate for describing a procedure where each step follows the previous one.)

   a. First . . .   b. At this point . . .   c. At the first stage . . .
      To begin with, . . .   After this . . .   At the second stage . . .
      Next . . .   At the third stage . . .
      Then . . .
      Later, . . .
      Finally . . .

2. Indicating Main Points

   (These are appropriate for listing things such as reasons, advantages and disadvantages, risks and benefits.)

   a. Firstly, . . .   b. Furthermore, . . .   c. One reason . . .
      Secondly, . . .   In addition, . . .   Another reason . . .
      Thirdly, . . .   Moreover, . . .   A further reason . . .
                                                   The final reason . . .

3. Indicating Cause and Effect

As a result, ...

As a consequence, ...

Consequently, ...

Therefore, ...

Due to ...

Because ...

4. Indicating Comparison and Contrast

In the same way, ...

Similarly, ...

In contrast, ...

On the one hand, ...

On the other hand, ...

Example

Topic Sentence: If you watch an artist paint a picture using water-colours, you will realise that it is important to follow a special procedure in order to achieve good results.

Explanatory Sentences: *To begin with*, the artist often sketches the scene in pencil. *Then*, before starting to paint, the artist wets the paper (to prevent the paper wrinkling up later when it dries). When he or she begins to paint, the artist always paints in the light colours first. *Later* the artist adds the darker colours.

Notice the transition words and phrases indicating time relationships are used here in this writing.

Exercise 4

Fill in the blanks in the following passages with proper transition words and phrases: (with possible answers)

(1)   We tend to take the postal service for granted. But when you think about it, getting a letter from A to B is quite a complicated process. _____, the letter is posted at a letter box. _____ it is collected by a mail van and taken to a sorting centre. Here it is sorted — either by hand or by machine — into the postal area of its destination.

152

_____, the letter and all the other letters for that area, are taken to the sorting centre for that area. Here it is sorted again before given to the postman or woman responsible for delivering the mail to a particular subdivision of that area.

(2)   It is now widely accepted that excessive consumption of refined sugar is not good for us. _____, refined sugar lacks nutrients and is, _____, not really a food. _____, refined sugar tends to be retained by the body in the form of fat. _____, although sugar initially gives us more energy, it can also contribute to the condition known as hypoglycaemia, or low blood sugar levels, leading to loss of energy. _____, of course, refined sugar is a major contributor to tooth decay.

(3)   Being a police officer has its good side and its bad side. _____, you feel as though you are making a contribution to the good of the community. Also you meet a lot of people, many of them quite fascinating. _____, although the people you meet are often interesting, they can also be pretty nasty. You have to face the violence and selfishness of people and their rudeness.

(4)   Economic recessions are cyclical in nature and are the result of a number of factors working on one another.

For example, a period of prosperity often leads to an over-production of goods and services. In other words, there are too many goods and services and not enough people wanting to buy them.

_____ manufactures then cut back production and some firms even go out of business. This causes unemployment which, in turn, brings about even lower demand _____ there are now fewer people who can afford to buy the goods and services.

_____, a vicious circle is set up leading to deeper and deeper recession in the economy.

(5)   The following is a description of how a television broadcast is made of a football game.

_____, several cameras are used. Each camera gives a different picture of the game. At the same time, a commentator describes the game. He or she speaks into a microphone.

_____, a television camera changes the picture into electric signals. These electric signals (vision signals) are sent to the television studio centre. The microphone converts the sound into another set of electric signals (sound signals). These sound signals are also sent to the television centre.

_____, the producer, at the studio centre, watches the pictures from each camera and listens to the commentator. He chooses the best picture. Then the programme is sent out from the television centre.

_____, the sound and vision signals are sent to the transmitting station.

5. Writing a Conclusion
(写结尾)

Essays should not finish abruptly with the last main point. The final paragraph should provide a conclusion. The concluding paragraph should be short and forceful and made up mainly of restatements or summaries of the points that have been discussed. Sometimes it is good to

1. link the concluding paragraph to the introduction, and
2. make recommendations.

In the concluding paragraph, you should not put in a summary of all your supports or everything in detail. That makes the essay repetitive and very boring to read.

You should not put in any new ideas in the concluding paragraph. If a new idea occurs in the conclusion, the reader may turn the page, expecting clarification and proof of the idea. In writing the concluding paragraph some phrases can be used:

1. For Summarising:	2. For Concluding:
In short, ...	In conclusion, ...
In a word, ...	On the whole, ...
In brief, ...	Altogether, ...
To sum up, ...	In all, ...

In the IELTS, two or three sentences should be considered enough for the concluding paragraph. Sometimes one sentence would do the job. See the following examples:

Example 1

In conclusion, if you want to travel, have a good time, spend money on yourself, it's best to stay single.

Example 2

At this stage, the process of letter sorting is completed.

Example 3

On the whole, although there is some evidence for the role of physiology in determining the dominance of black athletes in some American sports, sociological factors appear more influential.

Example 4

In short, at various times of their lives, people have different needs. While purchasing a home is often the best choice for somebody with an adequate income, for the reasons discussed, it is often not the most feasible choice for young foreign students.

5.1. Link the Concluding Paragraph to the Introduction (结尾与导语相应)

In some essays the concluding paragraph, in some way, is always connected with the introduction. It reaffirms the point of view put forward, or answers the question raised, in the introductory paragraph. Study the following examples:

Example 1

Introductory Paragraph:
An essay writing normally involves the following five stages.

Concluding Paragraph:
If you follow these five well-organized writing stages, your essay writing would be successful.

Example 2

Introductory Paragraph:
The diagram illustrates the circulation of the blood on by-pass through a heart-lung machine.

Concluding Paragraph:
The oxygenator, which gives the blood the oxygen which the body needs, is also part of the heart-lung machine. The blood, filled

156

with oxygen,　flows　through the plastic tube to the pump. At this stage the　circulation　starts all over again.

Example 3

Introductory Paragraph:

From time to time the question of state aid to denominational schools is raised and various forms of aid are demanded. At the moment we are being asked to consider the proposal that church schools should receive direct grants from the state, grants varying in amount according to the number of children in the school.

Concluding Paragraph:

In view of my remarks, it must be clear that we should oppose the demands of those who seek state grants for denominational schools: their case is a weak one, and their suggestions, if implemented, could have very dangerous consequences.

Example 4

Introductory Paragraph:

In the pursuit of scientific and technological progress, the mankind are facing more and more risks than before. Should we accept these risks or failures in the development of human science and technology? There are some reasons for us to challenge the risks.

Concluding Paragraph:

In conclusion, it is important for people to accept the risks in the pursuit of scientific and technological progress. What we must do is to study all the science subject intensively in order to avoid the reoccurring of risks.

Exercise 1

Read the following introductory paragraphs and body of the essays. Write a concluding paragraph for each of these essays. Your concluding paragraph should be in some way connected with the introductory paragraph. (with possible answers)

(1)

Recently the school leaving age was raised to fifteen years. I think all young people should stay at school until they are eighteen years old, not fifteen.

(Body)

The reasons for this are so obvious that it should be a matter of urgency for the government to make arrangements to implement such a policy immediately. The arguments advanced for the leaving age of fifteen were based on the benefits to be gained for the individual, and therefore for our society, and on the fact that our economy could afford the extra year. If these arguments are valid, then still greater benefits would accrue from extending formal education even further. The question of cost does not really arise, as we discovered in the last war, when we spent over a million pounds a day on defence.

Each year about Christmas time, thousands of adolescents of about fifteen or sixteen are looking for jobs, and many of them are unable to find suitable occupations. Keep them at school and this difficulty would be overcome immediately. Under the wise guidance of teachers the problems of juvenile delinquency would disappear. School work, libraries and community services would replace the football outer, the hotels and the milk bars.

(Concluding Paragraph)

. . .

(2)

(Introductory Paragraph)

It is essential that passengers follow a number of regulations before and during flight and in the event of emergencies.

(Body)

Before take-off, passengers should read the safety card in the seat pocket. They should also check the location of the emergency exits and the life jackets.

During the flight, seat belts should be kept fastened at all times when passengers are seated. Hand luggage must not be left in the aisles.

The following regulations apply in the case of emergencies. If the aircraft decompresses, cigarettes should be extinguished immediately and oxygen masks should be placed over the mouth and nose. In the event of an emergency landing, passengers should place their heads on their knees and their hands over their heads. They should then await instructions.

(Concluding Paragraph)

...

(3)

A proverb says : "Time is money." But in my opinion, time is even more precious than money. Because when money is spent, we can earn it back. But, when time is gone, it will never return. This is the reason why we must value time.

(Body)

It goes without saying that the time at our disposal is unusually limited. Hence, even an hour is extremely precious. We should make full use of our time to do useful things. As students we must not relax our efforts to engage in our studies so as to serve society and our nation in the future.

But it is a pity that there are a lot of people who do not know the importance of time. They spend their precious time smoking, drinking and gambling. They do not realize that wasting time is equal to wasting a part of their valuable life.

(Concluding Paragraph)

...

(4)

(Introductory Paragraph)

Overseas students who wish to be admitted to a British university require two documents: an acceptance advice form from the university and a visa from a British consular office.

(Body)

In order to do this, a student must first obtain, fill out and return an application form to the university where he or she wishes to study. This form should include academic examination and English language test results.

Successful applicants receive an acceptance advice form. On accepting the offer, the student must pay fees for the first half-year and then apply for a visa from a British consular office.

(Concluding Paragraph)

...

(5)

(Introductory Paragraph)

Some people claim that school uniforms take away some of the students' individuality and freedom, but it is quite possible for children to wear school uniforms and still be free individuals. I think school uniforms are an excellent idea and all schools should adopt them.

(Body)

Nothing looks nicer than to see all the children in a school neatly and tidily dressed. People who dislike school uniforms are really only expressing a personal opinion when they say they think children look better as a group when they are dressed differently.

I remember a school where I introduced school uniforms and the tone of the school and the conduct of the children improved remarkably. I noticed it myself and people in the district also commented on it to me. If children are allowed to dress in any old thing they please, they look like a mob and the effect is terrible. Also some of the girls start wearing jeans or slacks in winter, which shows they are poor types, and then others decide to copy them.

If everybody has to wear exactly the same clothes, nobody will be able to dress much more expensively than the others, so uniforms are very democratic. Also, they help children realize that they really belong to a school and are not just single individuals. Anyhow, they have plenty of opportunity to dress according to their own tastes, or their parents'tastes, outside school hours.

(Concluding Paragraph)

. . .

5.2. Make Recommendations (提建议)

In the IELTS, some writing tasks require the candidates to make some necessary recommendations. The concluding paragraph is the only place to put recommendations.

Example

Task: *Write a report for your sponsoring agency describing the English language skills overseas students are required of. Make any recommendations you feel are necessary.*

Concluding Paragraph:

It is important to acknowledge that most overseas students have difficulty in acquiring the language skills in writing, reading, speaking and listening. One way of overcoming these difficulties is to attend the language and study-skills classes which most institutions provide throughout the academic year. Another basic strategy is to find a study partner with whom it is possible to identify difficulties, exchange ideas and provide support.

Exercise 2

Write a conclusion for the following questions:
(1) What are the benefits and risks associated with the use of air-conditioning in hospitals? Make any recommendations you feel necessary.
(2) What are the advantages and disadvantages of studying abroad? Make any recommendations you feel necessary.
(3) Describe the most important adjustments to language learning styles you feel overseas students are likely to need to make and make any recommendations on how they should do this.
(4) Write a report to your sponsoring agency describing the accommodation problems faced by foreign students in Britain. Make any necessary recommendations.

6. Checking the Writing
(检查写作)

This final stage is very important for a writing test. Some mistakes can often be found and corrected by quickly checking through after you have finished writing. So you should make sure that you can leave yourself a short time (two to three minutes for task 1 and four to five minutes for task 2) to check your writing. You should use the time particularly to check that you have used correct spelling and grammar. The diagnostic tests in Part Two will help you to identify weakness you may have in spelling and grammar. You should pay particular attention to those areas when checking your writing.

6.1. Checking the Spelling (检查拼写)

The purpose of this section is to help you examine some of the common spelling mistakes made by the Chinese students when they are taking the English writing tests. Among these spelling mistakes two kinds of words are obvious. They are double letter words and silent letter words.

Example

1. Double Letter Words

abbreviate	rubbish	accelerate	accept
accommodation	according	occupation	occurred
succeed	address	efficient	effort
sufficient	traffic	exaggerate	luggage
suggest	challenge	collect	pollution
beginning	apparatus	appearance	opposite
arrange	impossible	necessary	attitude

2. Silent Letter Words

climb	doubt	design	foreigner
knife	knock	knowledge	psychology

receipt   wrap   writing   written

Exercise 1

1. Read the following sentences and try to find and correct the spelling mistakes in the sentences:
    (1) He bandoned his wife and childrern.
    (2) The driver stoped the taxi so abruply that his head was hit against the window.
    (3) The new tourist hotel will have accomodations for more than one sousand people.
    (4) While the Hill family was on vocation, their mail acumulated in the box.
    (5) Sunshine and fresh air acelerate a person's recuvery from sickness.
    (6) Although he was allmost ninety years old, he was still active and allert.
    (7) The directions were so ambigous that it was imposible to complete the asignment.
    (8) We must asume he has arived, but we don't know.
    (9) He was on his best behaivior becouse he wanted to impress his girl friend's family.
    (10) Your coffee is biter because you forgot to put suger in it.
    (11) The game was canciled because of the rain.
    (12) Mr. Wang is a colleage of Mr. Li.
    (13) She recives many complaments on her taste in clothes.
    (14) While he was so conffident that he had pasted the exam that he did not even bother to check the answer sheet.
    (15) I always take the bus to work because the congeston in the city makes it dificult to find a parking place.
    (16) The dilema is weather to lower the price or to accept fewer sales.
    (17) I am very doutful about signing this contracte because I am not sure about some of the fine points.
    (18) The durration of the examinaition is three hours.
    (19) Perhaps if you took vitamines you would have more emergy.
    (20) It is esential that you have these transcripts translated and notarized.
    (21) Unfortunately, all eforts to rescue the survivors were futil.
    (22) Although he did not say so directly, he impllied that he would be able to help us.
    (23) More than five billion people inhabite the earth.

163

(24) Some of the inovations on display at the World Science Fair will not be practical until the twenty-first centery.

(25) In this province, every car must be inspacted anually by the highway patrol.

(26) He does his work with such invarible accuracy that it is never necesary to make any corrections.

(27) The bullet penertrated the victim's chest and lodged itself just to the right of his heart.

(28) I have had several summer jobs but I have never been permernently employed.

(29) The baseball game will be postboned until next Monday because of rain.

(30) As soon as she learns the office rutine she will be an excelent assistant.

2. Read the following paragraphs and try to find and correct the spelling mistakes in the paragraphs:

(1) Fear is one of the emotions which form the comon human experience, and which rule the lives of men and the higher animels. It is a sound natral instinct aimed at self-preservation, bordered on the one hand by rational prudence, and by lame cowardice on the other; but since its roots lie in biological expediency, it cannot sencibly be regarded as a purely moral subject.

(2) What the anthropologist does in the study of moral systems is to examine for perticular societies the ideas of right and rong that are held, and their social cercumstances. Consideration of material from some of the more primitive societies, and a contrast of it with Westen patterns, will help to bring out some of the basik moral aspects of social action.

(3) In ansient Greece athletic festivals were very important and had strong religious asociations. The Olympian athletic festival, held every four years in honour of Zeus, eventualy lost its local character and became first a national event, and then, after the rules against foreign competitors had been waived, internationel. No one knows exactly how far back the Olympic Games go, but some oficial records date from 776 B.C.

(4) I wish to protest against the sugestion that new commercial television stations should be licensed only on condition that they devote more of their viewing time to programmes of some definit "educational valu", and that existing commercial stations should only be alowed to have their licences renewed on this condition.

(5) It seems to be a general asumption that raising the school leaving age can bring the comunity as a whole, and the indeviduals composing it, nothing

but benefit. I submit, however, that more harm than benefit results from im-creasing the age of compulsory atendance at school.

(6) The system of trial by jury is comonly regarded as esential to proper judicial procedure: it is part of the heritage of British justise, and the belief is widespred that the verdict of twelve average people selected at random from the street is likely to be a fair one. But I believe this system is unsatisfactary.

3. Read the following passages and try to find and correct the spelling mistakes:

Passage 1

Refuse sorting involves two major proceses: separation and colection.

Waste of various kinds including, for example, glass, food and ruber, is placed on a conveyor belt which first passes through a shredder befor moving to a primary air classifier. This classifier removes shedded paper and plastic and deposits them in a compactor. The remainning materials pass through a magnetic separator, which separates out steel cans and iron and deposits them into a collector.

Materials such as glass, food and non-ferrous metals are unable to pass through a trommel screen and are placed in a collector. Residual waste which passes through the trommel screen are then removed from the conveyor belt by a secondary air classifier.

At this stage all materials have been sorted and are readdy for recycling.

Passage 2

I shall atempt to convinse you that the place of women is in the home. The family is the unit of society and the mother is the centre of the family. How can the family keep together if the mother is out at work all day?

The goverment recognizes the need for women to be in the home by giv-ing taxation concessions for the housewife. Every year, we also celebrate Mother's Day with gifts and with songs and poems praising motherhood.

It can be sean that with the acelerating deterioration evident in family life today, the time is not far distant when, with the disapearance of the family, the human race will cease to exist.

In any case, women prefer to be at home. No person really wants to work. To be able to sit at home and gossip or read is every woman's ambi-tion. It would be a kindness to forbid women to work outside the home.

From these arguments, there can be no dout that society is best served when women are compeled to stay at home and look after their children.

6.2. Checking the Grammar (检查语法)

Within a short time you could not check everything about the grammar. You should concentrate on those grammatical points which you are likely to use incorrectly. You are suggested to check the use of prepositions and articles, the tenses and verbs. Do not try to correct the whole sentence or change the sentence structures at this stage. You will not have enough time to do so. In the following paragraph the words underlined should be corrected. The right answers are in the parentheses.

Example

When rain <u>fell</u> (falls) on mountains, it collects in depressions in the rock. The extreme cold <u>cause</u> (causes) the ice to freeze and glaciers to form. The ice melts and freezes again due to changes in temperature. Erosion of the rock of the mountain depression occurs as a result of the continual melting and refreezing, and <u>increased by</u> (is increased by) the action of wind moving the water. Eventually, the water wears away the rock enough to form a small stream which carries deposits of soil and rock which causes further erosion, gradually enlarging the stream bed. <u>A</u> (The) weather, too, acts on rocks and soil, to split, break and wear away. The stream grows larger until eventually it reaches the old age stage. The silt from the river is deposited <u>through</u> (into) the sea, resulting in sandbars, spits and promontories.

Exercise 2

Read the following passages and try to find and correct the grammatical mistakes:

Passage 1
A microscope is a instrument which is used by scientists to magnify very small objects to make them visible.

The commonest type is the optical microscope. An optical microscope consists a lens tube, a slide platform, an object condenser and a metal frame. The lens tube contains a number of lenses, the most important of which are the ocular and objective lenses. The lenses are for magnifying the object. The slide platform contains of a number of clamps for holding the slides. The object condenser is composed of a lens and a diaphragm. The latter will be used to control the amount of light entering the lens tube. The frame is made up of two parts: a heavy base and a swivelling top.

The optical microscope is enough good for ordinary laboratory work but for research the much more powerful electron microscope is using.

Passage 2

Lecturing as a method of teaching is so frequent under attack today from educational psychologists and by students that some justification needs to retain it.

Critics believe that it results in passive methods of learning which tend to be less effective than those which fully engage the learner. They also maintain that students have not opportunity to ask questions and must all receive the same content at the same pace, that they are exposed only to one teacher's interpretation of subject matter which will inevitably be biased and that, anyway, few lectures rise above dullness. Nevertheless, in a number of inquiries this pessimistic assessment of lecturing as a teaching method proves not to be general among students although they do fairly often comment on poor lecturing techniques.

Students praise lectures which are clear, orderly synopses in which basic principles are emphasised but dislike too numerous digressions or lectures which consist on part of the contents of a textbook. Students of science subjects consider that a lecture is a good way to introduce a new subject, putting it in its context, or to present material not yet included in books. They also appreciate its value as a period of discussion of problems and possible solutions with their lecturer. They do not look for inspiration — this is more commonly mentioned by teachers — but arts students look for originality in lectures. Medical and dental students who reported on teaching methods, or specifically on lecturing, suggest that there should be fewer lectures or that, at the least, more would be unpopular.

Different groups of students have different views. The argument towards the advantages and disadvantages of the lecturing method is still over consideration.

Part Five：Sample Tests

（第五部分：模拟试题）

1. Sample Test Five
（模拟试题五）

WRITING TASK 1

You should spend about 20 minutes on this task.

Task:

As a class assignment you have been asked to describe a camera.

Describe a camera, and explain how it works.

You may use your own knowledge and experience in addition to the diagram.

You should write at least 150 words.

Your description should be:
1. relevant to the task, and
2. well organized.

Shutter release
button

Aperture settings

Lens
cover

Lens

Front of
viewfinder

Back view

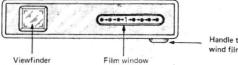

Viewfinder

Film window

Handle to
wind film

WRITING TASK 2

You should spend about 40 minutes on this task.

Task:

Write an essay for a university teacher on the following topic :

What are the advantages and/ or disadvantages brought to your particular situation by computers?

Give reasons for your answer

You should write at least 250 words.

You should use your own ideas, knowledge and experience and support your arguments with examples and relevant evidence.

In writing your essay, you should remember that:
1. the essay must be well organized
2. your point of view must be clearly expressed, and
3. your argument must be supported by relevant evidence.

2. Sample Test Six
（模拟试题六）

WRITING TASK 1

You should spend about 20 minutes on this task.

Schistosoma lives as a parasite in the water snail during one stage of its life-cycle, and in man during another stage as in the diagram below.

Task:

As a class assignment you have been asked to do the following task:

Write a short paragraph describing the life-cycle of schistosome, the parasite causing bilharzia.

You should write at least 150 words.

You may use your own knowledge and experience in addition to the diagram.

Your description should be:
1. relevant to the task, and
2. well organized.

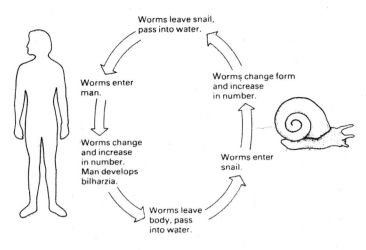

WRITING TASK 2

You should spend about 40 minutes on this task.

Task:

Write an essay for a university teacher on the following topic:

Should immunization be permitted in your country?
Give reasons for your answer.

You should write at least 250 words.

You should use your own ideas, knowledge and experience and support your arguments with examples and relevant evidence.

In writing your essay you should remember that:
1. your writing must be well organized
2. your point of view must be clearly expressed, and
3. your arguments must be supported by relevant evidence.

3. Sample Test Seven
（模拟试题七）

WRITING TASK 1

You should spend about 20 minutes on this task.

Task：

As a course assignment you are asked to write a description of the changes in the popularity of cinema and television from 1957 to 1974.

you should write at least 150 words.

You may use your own knowledge and experience in addition to the information in the graph.

Make sure your description is：
1. relevant to the question, and
2. well organized.

The changes in the popularity of cinema and television 1957–1974.

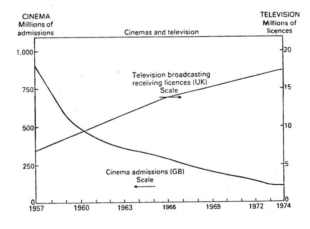

WRITING TASK 2

You should spend about 40 minutes on this task.

Task:

Write an essay for a university teacher on the following topic:

To what extent has the women's social position changed over the past 20 *years? What recommendations could you make to improve the current situation?*

Give reasons for your answer.

You should write at least 250 words.

You should use your own ideas, knowledge and experience and support your arguments with examples and relevant evidence.

In writing your essay you should remember that:
1. your writing must be well organized
2. your point of view must be clearly expressed, and
3. your arguments must be supported by relevant evidence.

4. Sample Test Eight
（模拟试题八）

WRITING TASK 1

You should spend about 20 minutes on this task.

Task：

    A friend who lives abroad will shortly be visiting your university and has asked you to make arrangements for his stay. Write a letter informing him of what you have done.

You should write at least 150 words.

You do NOT need to write your own address.

Begin your letter as follows：

IALS
University of Edinburgh,
21 *Hill Place,* EH8 9DP

Dear . . . ,

WRITING TASK 2

You should spend about 40 minutes on this task.

Task：

    Write a report to your course supervisor. Explain briefly what course you want to take abroad and what qualifications you hope to get, and what you hope to do with these qualifications when you return to your own country.

You should write at least 250 words.

Key to the Exercises and Sample Writings*

（练习答案及范文）

* All the sample writings are kept as they were. The mistakes in the writing are indicated in italics and possible corrections for them are provided at the end of each passage.

Part One: Sample Tests
(第一部分：模拟试题)

Sample Test One（模拟试题一）

Writing Task 1:

Describe an automatic electric oven, and explain how it works.

Sample Writing 1: (Score: 8)

An automatic electric oven is a device for baking bread and cooking food at home.

It mainly consists of four parts, namely, the oven body, the heaters, the door and the cooking control system. Of these parts, the heaters are the key components which use electricity to produce heat through resistor coils. The heat, in turn, is used to operate the appliance.

The oven works as follows: first, the food on the oven plates is placed on the grills which should be fixed to the racks inside the oven, and *close the door*, the attachment plug then may be connected to the power socket. Afterwards, press the heater switch and the oven begins to work which can be indicated by the cooking lamp. The desired amount of heat supplied to the oven can be controlled automatically by the cooking timer dial and temperature control dial connected to the electric circuits that switch the currents on and off. When the fixed time is up, the baked food can be taken out.

For the practical reason of saving time and personal effort, the automatic electric oven is now entering thousands of *families* and becoming one of the favourite household electric appliances for average families.

close the door: next close the door
families: homes

Sample Writing 2: (Score: 7)

The following diagram shows the structure of an automatic electric oven.
It mainly consists of three *parts*, the body, the door and the heating system.

178

Inside the body, there are racks for supporting oven plates and grills. The door includes the finder and the door handle. The heating system is roughly composed of the upper and lower *heater*, the temperature control dial, the cooking time dial, the heater switch, the cord, the attachment plug, etc.

When food is being cooked, it is put on *oven* plate inside the oven and the door is firmly closed. By attaching the plug with electric source and turning on the heater switch, the food is heated. The temperature control dial helps setting suitable cooking temperature, and the cooking timer dial is used to choose the proper cooking time. The cooking lamp on the other hand indicates whether the food is ready or not.

The oven is convenient for family cooking.

parts, : parts:
heater: heaters
oven: an oven

Sample Writing 3: (Score: 6)

The following picture shows us an automatic electric oven.

Its shape is cubic and it consists of three parts: the door covered with finder on the front, the upper and lower heaters which heat the food and the cooking control system which realizes the automatic cooking function.

When you use the automatic electric oven to cook *some food*, you must do the following things. Firstly, you have to put the food *to* the oven plate, open the front door, push the plate into the oven and then close it. Secondly, you have to use the temperature control dial and the cooking temperature and cooking time *are concerned with* the kind of the food. Finally, when the cooking finishes, the cooking lamp will show it.

This is the structure of the automatic electric oven and how it works.

Its shape: The shape of the oven
some food: food
to: on
are concerned with: depend on

Writing Task 2:

How much risk is acceptable in the pursuit of scientific and technological progress?

Sample Writing 1: (Score: 8)

As we know, everything in the world has its own two sides. Without exception, scientific and technological progress has brought us not only benefits but also risks. But now how much risk can be acceptable in the pursuit of scientific and technological progress to us?

It is very clear that scientific and technological progress has already brought us enormous benefits in all aspects of society, *which greatly promote* our social development. The invention of steam engine, for example, gave rise to the industrial revolution, which considerably increased the productivity. The use of modern medicine, such as penicillin, has saved millions of lives.

However, it cannot be denied that some risks have unavoidably occurred *accompanying* with the scientific and technological progress. One example is the explosion of the space shuttle, Challenger. The whole world was shocked and saddened by the loss of seven excellent astronauts, which seemed so difficult to accept. With the development of industry, plenty of products meet our needs, meanwhile serious environmental pollution occurs, which goes against our diligent pursuit of improving the quality of life. To these problems what can we do? We should take more efficient measures to avoid and minimize these risks.

On the whole, although some risks occur and are difficult to accept, the benefits outweigh the risks provided by scientific and technological progress in any sense, otherwise, our society would not go forward.

which greatly promote: which has greatly promoted
accompanying: along

Sample Writing 2: (Score: 7)

In the pursuit of scientific and technological progress, the mankind are facing more and more risks than before. Should we accept these risks or failures in the development of human science and technology? There are some reasons for us to challenge the risk.

The first reason to accept the risk is that *society civilization* needs scientific and technological progress. In the long period of human development, it is often true that scientific and technological progress makes every jumping in technological revolution. We cannot stop the developing of civilization just for fear of the risk.

The second reason *is lied* in the fact that the risk is usual and common when people step into an unknown area. For example, on May 6th, 1937, the world's largest airship, the Hindenburg, broke into flames in its floating. The result is serious and 35 people were dead. It is, however, necessary for us to continue the developing because we can learn the lesson and find the *reason* of failure. It is said that failure is the mother of success.

In conclusion, it is important for people to accept the risk in the pursuit of scientific and technological progress. What we must do is to study all the science subjects intensively in order to avoid the reoccurring of *risk*.

society civilization: civilization
is lied: lies
reason: cause
risk: failure

Sample Writing 3: (Score: 6)

With the development of science and technology progress, there were some kinds of *risks occurred*, and in some cases, it may be quite serious. However, mankind should not postpone their pursuit *to* the progress of science and technology.

Man's history proved that there were always some kinds of risks in their tests to an advanced level. The explosion of the Hindenburg can be a good example. But man learnt a lot from this. After this accident, man developed an airship by using some non-burning gas, and then it *gets more safty*, and the new type of airship has been used nowadays for a variety of *uses*.

Another thing that should be pointed out is that although the development of science and technology brings something which is not good for human beings, man can deal with them better and better. For instance, the development of industry brings world wide pollution problems, but with the development of environment technology man has begun to pay much more attention to this *affairs* and a lot of measures have been taken and, a lot of experts believe that environmental problems could be solved if a world-wide *attention being payed*.

In conclusion, man should not stop their *running after to* progress in science and technology although there are some risks in doing so. Mankind, however, should be aware of the risk brought by them, and take effective measures to reduce the risk to a minimum extent.

risks occurred: risks

to: of

gets more safty: became safer

uses: purposes

affairs: problem

attention being payed: effort is made

running after to: pursuit for

Sample Test Two（模拟试题二）

Writing Task 1:

As a class assignment your tutor has asked you to write about a heart-lung machine. Using the diagram below, write three or four paragraphs describing the circulation of the blood on by-pass through a heart-lung machine.

Sample Writing 1:（Score: 8）

The diagram illustrates the circulation of the blood on by-pass through a heart-lung machine.

Firstly the plastic tubes from the heart-lung machine to the patient are connected. Then the operator of the machine starts the pump. When the pump is going steadily at the right speed, the patient's heart and the machine are sharing the work of pumping the blood round the body. At this stage, the surgeon stops the supply of blood to the heart, and the machine alone controls the circulation. The patient is now "on by-pass".

The pumping operation itself is usually done by a roller passing over a section of the plastic tube and it needs very careful and accurate adjustment. The temperature of the blood drops as it passes through the tubes and the machine, because the room temperature is lower than the body's, *so* the machine includes a device for heating the blood before it returns to the body. Before the heated blood returns to the body it goes through the filter to pass bubbles of oxygen through the blood.

The oxygenator, which gives the blood the oxygen which the body needs, is also part of the heart-lung machine. The blood, filled with oxygen, flows through the plastic tube to the pump. At this stage the circulation starts all over again.

so: and so

182

Sample Writing 2: (Score: 7)

The heart-lung machine is used for maintaining the circulation of blood supply during a patient's operation, which by-passes and takes over the functions of the heart and the lungs.

The machine mainly consists of a pump, a temperature regulator, an oxygenator, a filter and plastic tubes. Of these, the oxygenator is a very important device which serves to oxygenate the blood.

As the blood leaves the vessels of the heart, it flows down a plastic tube until it enters the oxygenator. It is partly filled with blood, where the blood absorbs oxygen. Then, the oxygenated blood is pumped to the heart regulator where the temperature of blood can be adjusted properly. After passing through the filter for bubbles, the blood finally supplies to the stopped heart and lungs. *Another following* blood circulation begins again.

Another following: Another

Sample Writing 3: (Score: 6)

The following picture shows the circulation of the blood on by-pass through a heart-lung machine.

The heart-lung machine mainly consist of five parts: the plastic tubes, the oxygenator, the pump, the equipment which can make the blood warmer, and the filter. All the parts above take an important part in the circulation of the blood on by-pass through a heart-lung machine.

The heart-lung machine works as follows:

When the heart needs to be operated on, the heart's work should be stopped and the blood in *heart* should be moved out by plastic tubes. At this time, *the oxygenator serves as the lung, which receives the blood from the heart stopped and adds with oxygen to it*. And then *move the blood to pump which functions like a heart*. Pumping blood is pushed by turning the roller on it. While the blood is heated, it passes through the filter so that the bubbles in the blood are taken away. Finally the blood is supplied to each organ and tissue of the whole body and *maintain the body's normal activity*. Meanwhile, *make the operation* smoothly.

heart: the heart
the oxygenator... to it: the oxygenator functions and adds oxygen to the

blood as the lung, which receives the blood from the heart, stopped.
move... a heart: move the blood to the pump which functions like a heart
maintain the body's normal activity: the body's normal activity is maintained
make the operation: the operation could go

Writing Task 2:

"Education about diet is the most essential feature of a country's health-care programme." Is this a justified assumption?

Sample Writing 1: (Score: 8)

"Education about diet is the most essential feature of a country's health-care programme." But some people are doubtful about this assumption. Some justifications, therefore, should be made.

First of all, people would be aware of the importance of diet through education. A country's health-care programme cannot be successful without people's knowing it.

Next, even if people know the importance of diet, they often do not know how to keep a proper diet. Accordingly, it is essential to let people understand the appropriate approaches of diet through education.

Finally, education is a basic link of the chain to carry out the country's health-care programme. Before any actions are taken, the government should tell their *citizens* the significance of the programme and the measures to fulfil it. Through education, the programme can become *people's activities*. As a result, the government can reach their goal to promote their *citizens'* health level.

In conclusion, it is an essential feature to implement a country's health-care programme through education about diet. In addition, other meassures and actions should also be followed.

   citizens: people
   people's activities: the people's activities
   citizens': people's

Sample Writing 2: (Score: 7)

We all know that there are different habits for diet in different areas. However, some diet habits are harmful to our health. Therefore, education for diet is
184

necessary.

It is really true that most of the people in some areas suffer from various diseases or *are not* long life due to bad diet habits. For instance, in Northern Ireland, people have a fancy for eating fried food, such as fried potatoes, eggs and bacon. As a result, many people suffer from high blood pressure and heart disease, and pass away early. Thus, we cannot say that a good diet habit is not important.

Furthermore, we cannot deny the fact that some people place special emphasis on high proteins, but ignore the importance of vegetables and fruits on health. Keeping a health needs not only proteins but also various vitamines from vegetables and fruits. To some extent, vegetables and fruits are more important to long life than proteins. For example, it has been reported that people in some mountain areas *only eating* vegetables without any meat can live over a hundred years. It is quite clear that knowledge on diet and health is very important.

In conclusion, if we want to keep good health, we must *emphasis the* good diet habit.

> are not: do not live a
> only eating: eating only
> emphasis the: follow a

Sample Writing 3: (Score: 6)

Every country has its own specific customs on diet. In order to impove people's health-care, what should we do?

It is clear that some specific customs on diet in a country have been formed for a long time. Although such diet benefits a lot to the people, it cannot be denied that some diets have brought to us some kinds of *disease*. That is to say that some diets are related to some kinds of diseases. A survey demonstrates that half the chronic *disease* in U.S.A. *is* related to diet, alcohol and smoking. In Northern Ireland heart attacks related to their breakfast diet are a far more lethal and real threat than any fights. While in Asia, the diet seems to help prevent chronic diseases. To cope with this problem, what should we do?

Our answer is that education about diet is essential. In a family, parents may affect their children's diet. If parents are the perfect role models, their children may learn from them and avoid some kinds of bad *diet* such as smoking. In school and the society, we can educate people to form a good diet in order to prevent some diseases. *Doing so*, we can achieve some good results.

To sum up, education about diet is an effective measure in health-care programme to compete with the disease.

disease：diseases
disease：diseases
is：are
diet：diet habits
Doing so：By doing so

Sample Test Three （模拟试题三）

Writing Task 1：

The diagram below illustrates a patterned plan of essay writing. Write three or four paragraphs to describe the plan and consider whether any changes are necessary.

Sample Writing 1：（Score：8）

An essay writing normally involves the following five stages.

The first stage is analyzing the task. That is to say that you should analyse what the topic is, what the purpose is, what the requirements are, etc.

The second stage is preparing a plan. At this stage, an outline of writing should be made which normally includes the introduction, body and conclusion.

The third stage is collecting relevant information. The relevant information includes the information provided and your own knowledge.

The fourth stage is writing up. This is the central part. Based on the above information, you can write the essay now.

The last stage is checking your writing. This requests you to check your whole essay especially in grammar, spelling and handwriting. Although this is the final step, you cannot ignore it at all.

If you follow the well-organized writing steps, your *writing essay* would be successful.

An essay：Essay
writing essay：writing / essay writing

Sample Writing 2：（Score：7）

The description below is a patterned plan of essay writing.

186

First of all, the essay task should be analyzed carefully. The failure of this step will cause the essay to mislead.

The next step is to prepare *a plan of the writing*. *To do well in this stage* will benefit the following writing.

The third step is to collect some relevant information to fulfil the essay. The paper will not be attractive or persuasive unless it has a lot of *content* .

The fourth step, the most important step, is to write up. *Writer* will finish his essay in this stage. All the plans and ideas will get realized.

The last step is to check the writing. This step is necessary because there is little writing without any mistakes.

In all the steps, it should be pointed out that the fourth step should be emphasized obviously.

The process of essay writing has been described as above.

a plan of the writing: a writing plan
To do well in this stage: To do this well
content: relevant content
Writer: The writer

Sample Writing 3: (Score: 6)

The diagram below shows a patterned plan of essay writing.

First of all, the task of writing is analyzed. This generally includes the recognition of the topic and issue of the task.

Secondly, relevant information is collected. In doing this, classification of *the information* is also made so that it is ready for writing up.

Writing up is considered to be the most important part, because it occupies *largest part of*. Writing should be as clear, *logic* as possible.

The last part of writing is to check what you have done. In this part usually we only concentrate on spelling and grammar. No essential changes should be made here because *the limited time*.

The above writing plan is considered suitable for most essay writing, no changes on it seem to be necessary.

the information: information
largest part of: most of the part
logic: logical
the limited time: of the time limitation

Writing Task 2:

Discuss the question of the death penalty in general.
How far do you think it is justified?

Sample Writing 1: (Score: 8)

Death penalty is a question of controversy. People have different notions about the matter: some uphold it as necessary, others *condemn* as "murder by the state". Therefore, I would like to have a look at the question in this essay to decide how justifiable death penalty could be.

One of the strong points is that it is a necessary measure to maintain social order. In other words, social civilization is based on a well-formed system which stipulates that there are things we, as members of a society, can do, and things we are not supposed to do, such as deliberate murder. If one violates the system, then he has to pay for it — sometimes to forfeit his own life. Moreover, though most people find it difficult to accept the fact that a state should execute a murderer, it is virtually fair enough if we look at the matter from the point of view of the victim and his/her family. In fact, it is equally difficult for the family to accept the fact that their relatives died for something which should not have happened at all. That is to say death penalty is a way to guarantee social order and punish those who fail to comply with the law.

On the other hand, the opponents of death penalty tend to take the matter more emotionally. For example, in China some people feel that putting a murderer to death will not bring the victim back to life again. They actually share with the opinion of some people *who, believing* that death penalty is too inhuman. Though their feeling is understandable in a sense, we really cannot let our feeling make a judgement on a matter of life and death. If that happened, we would not be able to maintain justice in our society and consequently civilization would be undermined.

In conclusion, I would like to say that it is extremely necessary and crucial to maintain death penalty in our society. Without it, it is hard to keep our civilization complete. However, I do believe that death penalty should be carefully handled. Each case should be thoroughly reviewed and concluded on the basis of facts. Only in this way can the purpose of death penalty be fulfilled and justice maintained.

condemn: condemn it
who, believing: who believe

188

Sample Writing 2: (Score: 7)

According to the opinion of some people, there are quite different attitudes towards the death penalty. Although some claimed that death penalty is "barbarous", it is quite necessary to use death penalty against heinous crimes.

First, death penalty is quite necessary because it is the need of *social order maintaining* . It is an effective anti-crime measure to the heinous crimes such as rape, kidnapping, robbery and so on. Without it, more people would be murdered or hurt, and heinous crimes would increase.

Second, human's life is very valuable. Once a man is killed, he would not return to life again. The one who murdered others should give his own life as a punishment, which is fair enough.

Finally, death penalty is a consolation to the victim's relatives. Just imagine what a sorrowful feeling they would have to their son or daughter's unexpected death.

To sum up, the *penalty of death* is quite necessary to maintain social order. But it also needs *to stress* that the death penalty is a question of life or death, so it should be carefully handled and only used to those "heinous crimes".

social order maintaining: maintaining social order

penalty of death: death penalty

to stress: to be stressed

Sample Writing 3: (Score: 6)

Some people say human life is sacred and even if a person *commits law of murder* he should not be killed. So the question arises whether death penalty is right or not.

It is true that misuse of death penalty may result in disaster. For example, some wrong judgement may lead to innocent person losing his invaluable *life and even when the fact is clear* .

However, in some cases, such as to a crazy killer, if death penalty is forbidden *to use* , it is quite possible for him to kill more people. In this case, It is dangerous without death penalty.

Next, death penalty can be used as a warning. For example, in France, during the period when death penalty was canceled, the rate of crimes increased sharply. At least, death penalty can remind something when a criminal wants to commit the crime.

Finally, death penalty is a practical and economic solution to some dangerous murderers. It can prevent these criminals *escaping* , and save a lot of money and labour force for prison.

Therefore, we can not say that death penalty should be canceled. What we should do is to be careful when we use it.

commits law of murder: commits murder
life and even when the fact is clear: life
to use: to be used
escaping: from escaping

Sample Test Four （模拟试题四）

Writing Task 1:

Write to the Student Accommodation Office telling them what your situation is, what accomodation you wish to have and ask for any suggestions.

Sample Writing 1: (Score: 8)

Class 23, Chu Guo Bu
Beijing Language and
    Culture University
Beijing, 100083
P. R. China
May 26, 1996

Director
Student Accommodation Office
30 Buccleuch Place
Edinburgh EH8 9JS
U.K.

Dear Sir/Madam,

I am a Chinese student. In the coming October, I will go to your university to do cooperation research in the Department of Geography as a visiting scholar.

I have known from the booklet on accommodation in your university that I should apply for an accommodation in advance.

This time I am going to your university alone. The accommodation I prefer *is to get a small* furnished flat on the campus. If permitted, I'd like to share the flat with two male friends of mine who will go to your university along with me.

Now, would you be kind enough to get a flat with two bedrooms for me? If not possible, what kind of accommodation would you be able to offer to me?

Your kind help would be greatly appreciated.

I am looking forward to your early reply.

Yours sincerely,
(signature)
Zhang Li

is to get a small: is a small

Sample Writing 2: (Score: 7)

Box 108
Beijing Language and
Culture University
Beijing, 100083
26 May, 1996

Student Accommodation Office
30 Buccleuch Place,
Edinburgh EH8 9JS

Dear Sirs,

I am a visiting scholar from China. I will study in Edinburgh University for one year, so I would like to find a suitable accommodation near the campus of the university. *At same time*, I am going to get further understanding of the British life style as well as the language. Therefore I am writing to you and hope I could get help from you.

According to my situation. I am going to find a British family to live with, in this case I can eat with *them and share* the family facilities and, the most important, improve my *English level*. My friend told me that a bed sitter is also quite good and suitable for me. Which is better and easier to find, I would like to have your suggestions. I am looking forward to your reply.

Yours sincerely,
Chen Bing

At same time: At the same time

them and share: them, share

English level: English

Sample Writing 3: (Score: 6)

Class 22, Chu Guo Bu
Beijing Language and
    Culture University
Beijing, 100083
26 May, 1996

Student Accommodation Office
30 Buccleuch Place,
Edinburgh EH8 9JS

Dear Sir,

I am a Chinese student. I have received a letter from your university to accept me as an overseas student. So I decide to *come* to University of Edinburgh this September.

The aim which I am writting to your office is to ask for your help *in* my accommodation. I think I would prefer to live with a British family so as to have more opportunities to communicate with the local people and make friends with them. At the same time, I also want to improve my English. However, what I need *in* British family is a bed sitter, which costs about 25 pounds per week. The above is what I am thinking now. Maybe *there are some difficulties* to find this accommodation. Could you write back to me as soon as possible? I am looking forward to hearing from you soon.

Yours faithfully,
Li Ming

come: go

in: for

in: from a

there are some difficulties: it is difficult

Writing Task 2:

Write briefly what you have already done in your own field, and what you wish to do in the future course.

Sample Writing 1: (Score: 8)

In the field of economy, I have studied for more than ten years, and obtained some achievements. I wish I would study abroad to learn advanced *economic theory* and do some investigations.

My main achievements are reflected in my articles published in the Chinese academic periodicals. I have researched on population theory and put forward my viewpoints about this issue, which were highly regarded by the Chinese professors and scholars. *And at same time* , I have made a great deal of investigations on the state and problems of Chinese population and have made some suggestions.

I am going to continue my study and research abroad. I wish I could attend a course on population theory and grasp the Western principles and methods on this subject systematically. And if possible, I would like to join a research group to undertake a research attachment at a British university, so that I can have an opportunity to carry on some investigation and do comparative study.

My qualification seems suitable to be a scholar going abroad, and I am sure I will acquire greater achievements after studying in Britain.

economic theory: theory on economy
And at same time: And at the same time

Sample Writing 2: (Score: 7)

As an overseas scholar from China, I have written an application for one year's research attachment in Leeds University. To support this application, a few explanations on my option need to be made in the light of what I have done and what I am going to do.

I have been studying in the field of polymer materials for over ten years. During this period, I did several *works* in the area, for example, processing, structure and properties, crystalline and morphology of polymers. Recently I have been involved in the research of inner crystals detecting of polymer materials, in which a laser beam is used to test the material. This is also the most interesting work to me.

According to my background, I hope to expand my knowledge in the area of liquid crystalline polymer, *concentration* on its structure and property relationship. I believe that *study* in this area is most suitable for me and will be beneficial to my future work on my return.

On the whole, interests and background are the key factors which lead me to make the above choice.

works: projects
concentration: concentrating
study: studying

Sample Writing 3: (Score: 6)

I am working for Land Economy Institute of State Land Administration. My speciality is land economy.

In the *last* 6 years, I have published several books and papers about land economy and attended several international symposiums. *My greatest subject* I like best is China's urban land reform.

China's urban land reform has been carried out for 6 years. It is still in experimental and popularizing stage. During this stage, *we found* a lot of experience and lessons which are very useful to the further reform.

According to international experiences and China's situation, I shall focus on land market and land appraisal in the future. The developed countries all have a developed land market and advanced land appraisal technology. I have to study the knowledge of these countries and use the knowledge in China. I shall give the knowledge in China through training and *giving* lectures on TV. In the near future, China's land economy *which I have researched* will do great contributions to China's market economy.

last: past
My greatest subject: The subject
we found: we have found
giving: also give
which I have researched: which I have researched on

Part Two: Diagnostic Tests
（第二部分：诊断测试）

1. Test One: Spelling

1.1.

1. abandoned	2. children
3. stopped	4. abruptly
5. thousand	6. accelerate
7. recovery	8. almost
9. alert	10. ambiguous
11. impossible	12. assignment
13. assume	14. arrived
15. behaviour	16. because
17. cancelled	18. colleague; college
19. receives	20. confident
21. supervisor	22. lecturer
23. government	24. section
25. examination	26. proposal
27. contrary	28. opposite
29. system	30. infer
31. analysis	32. development
33. facilities	34. appropriate
35. knowledge	36. exceed
37. framework	38. progress
39. chronological	40. responsibility
41. resource	42. experiment
43. characterise	44. gradually
45. laboratory	46. parallel
47. psychological	48. concrete
49. criticism	50. pursuit
51. questionnaire	52. modification
53. distribution	54. describe
55. assignment	56. comparative
57. significant	58. sustainable

59. equipment

60. approaches

61. weakness

62. apparatus

63. approximately

64. measurement

65. decrease

66. sequential

67. observe

68. attempt

69. perspective

70. multiple

71. elementary

72. simultaneous

73. correlation

74. discussion

75. emphasize, emphasise

76. variability

77. involvement

78. belief

79. significance

80. recognise

81. summarise

82. synthesize, synthesise

83. separate

84. estimate

85. parameter

86. policy

87. inevitably

88. predominantly

89. material

90. efficiency

91. review

92. consumption

93. abundance

94. theoretical

95. graphic

96. achievement

97. receive

98. response

99. pattern

100. acquire

1.2.

1. congestion

2. dilemma

5. doubtful

8. duration

9. examination

10. vitamins

11. energy

14. essential

15. efforts

16. futile

18. century

22. annually

23. penetrated

24. permanently

27. postponed

28. routine

32. accommodation

33. achieve

37. applicable

38. beginning

39. college

43. correct

45. experimental

48. increasingly

49. insufficient

50. knowledge

53. maintaining

54. necessary

59. referring

60. research

62. studying	63. techniques
64. university	65. which
69. career; carrier	70. criticism
73. disappeared	74. emphasis
80. foreigner	86. interviewed
87. lovely	90. medicine
93. occupation	94. resources
99. thorough; through	100. whether; weather
106. writing	115. height
118. institute	120. successful

1.3.

1. stabilisation	n.	稳定
2. dramatically	ad.	戏剧性地
3. design	vt. & vi.	计划；谋划；设计；构思
	n.	计划；设计
4. continuous	a.	继续的
5. assessment	n.	估价
6. orientation	n.	定向
7. consider	vt.	考虑；细想；认为；把……看作
	vi.	考虑；细想
8. future	n.	将来
9. emission	n.	散发；发射
10. allocation	n.	分配
11. distribute	vt.	分发；分配；散布
12. limitation	n.	限制
13. concentration	n.	集中
14. adopt	vt.	采用；采纳；收养
15. assume	vt.	假定；设想；担任；承担；采取
16. diverse [dai'və:s]	a.	不一样的
17. vary	vt.	改变；变更
	vi.	变化；不同
18. lengthen	vt.	使延长
	vi.	变长；延伸
19. specify	vt.	指定；详细说明
20. produce	vt.	生产；产生；引起

197

		vi.	生产；创作
21.	author	n.	作者
22.	frequently	ad.	经常地
23.	configuration	n.	构造
24.	specification	n.	详述
25.	minor	a.	较小的
26.	phase	n.	阶段
27.	concern	vt.	涉及；对……有关系，影响；使关心
		n.	（利害）关系；关心
28.	depletion	n.	耗尽
29.	simulator	n.	模拟器
30.	sample	n.	样本
31.	per capita	n.	每人；人均
32.	relationship	n.	关系
33.	quantitative	a.	量的
34.	bibliography	n.	书目提要
35.	serve	vt.	为……服务；给……干活；招待
		vi.	服务；帮佣；招待
36.	role	n.	作用
37.	consistency	n.	坚固性；一致性
38.	quote	vt. & vi.	引用
39.	ensure	vt.	保证；保护
40.	edit	vt.	编辑；剪辑（影片、录音磁带等）
41.	employ	vt.	用；雇用；使忙于
42.	redundant	a.	过剩的
43.	irrelevant	a.	不相干的
44.	depth	n.	深度
45.	match	n.	比赛
46.	correspond	vi.	符合；一致；相当；相应；通信
47.	common	a.	通常的
48.	experience	n.	经验
49.	animal	n.	动物
50.	natural	a.	自然的
51.	instinct	n.	本能

52.	rational	a.	理性的
53.	prudence	n.	谨慎
54.	lame	a.	残废的
55.	cowardice ['kauədis]	n.	懦弱 coward ['kauəd] n.懦夫 a.懦夫的
56.	biological	a.	生物学的
57.	expediency [iks'pi:djənsi] n.		便利 a.明智的 n.判断力强的 sensible ['sensəbl]
58.	sensibly	ad.	明智地
59.	moral ['mərəl]	a.	道德的
60.	subject	n.	题目；学科
61.	anthropologist	n.	人类学家
62.	unsatisfactory	a.	不满意的
63.	particular	a.	特别的
64.	society	n.	社会
65.	circumstance	n.	情况
66.	consideration	n.	考虑
67.	primitive ['primitiv]	a.	原始的
68.	contrast	n.	对比；对照；不大相同的人（或物）
		vt.	使对比；使对照
		vi.	形成对照
69.	aspect	n.	样子；方面
70.	action	n.	行动
71.	ancient	a.	古代的
72.	athletic	a.	运动的
73.	religious	a.	宗教的
74.	association	n.	联合；协会
75.	festival	n.	节日
76.	honour	n.	荣誉
77.	eventually	ad.	终于
78.	character	n.	特性
79.	international	a.	国际的
80.	exactly	ad.	确切地
81.	protest	vt. & vi.	断言；主张；抗议；反对（against）
82.	suggestion	n.	建议
83.	commercial	a.	商业的
84.	television	n.	电视
85.	license	n.	牌照

86. condition	n.	条件
87. devote	vt.	把……奉献
88. programme	n.	节目；方案；程序
89. definite	a.	明确的
90. allow	vt.	允许；准许；允给；让……得到
	vi.	考虑到；顾及；体谅（for）；容许；容得（of）
91. assumption	n.	假定
92. justify	vt.	证明……是正当的（或有理的）；为……辩护
93. individual	a.	个人的
94. compose	vt.	组成；构成；创作（乐曲、诗歌等）；为（歌词等）作曲
	vi.	创作；作曲
95. benefit	n.	利益
96. submit	vt.	使服从；呈送；提交；提出；认为
	vi.	服从；屈服；忍受
97. compulsory	a.	义务的
98. attendance	n.	出席
99. proper	a.	合适的
100. commonly	ad.	通常地

1.4.

1. to convey ［kən'vei］ 传递，运送
2. to depress
3. outlet
4. output
5. outlook
6. to avoid
7. to concede
8. to consist of
9. to disrupt
10. obsolete a. ［'ɔbsəliːt］ 作废的，过时的
11. successive; continued; continous
12. serious
13. external; outside
14. internal; inside
15. interval
16. to enhance; to improve
17. to undertake
18. to undergo
19. to aggravate ［'æɡraveit］v.
20. aggression
21. liberty; freedom 使更坏
22. facilities; equipment

（俗）路怒，这惯

23. investigation
24. festival
25. mature
26. dot; point
27. to invert
28. identical
29. guilty
30. innocent
31. to vanish; to disappear
32. to disapprove; to disagree
33. behaviour
34. routine
35. efficiency
36. accuracy
37. accurate
38. to accomplish; to finish
39. efficient
40. emphasis
41. confident
42. adequate
43. to postpone
44. former
45. latter
46. interest
47. hesitation
48. to disconnect; to separate
49. climax ('klimæks) n.顶点. 高潮
50. consequently
51. precisely
52. nevertheless
53. ratio
54. species
55. specific
56. general
57. maximum
58. maximal
59. minimum
60. minimal
61. approximate
62. reliable
63. to interfere
64. chaos ('keips) n.混乱
65. chaotic   ('veipə)
66. crude
67. originally   Vapour
68. evaporate (i'væpəreit) v.蒸发. 消失
69. to be composed of
70. conjunction
71. to reinforce
72. membership
73. probability
74. inevitable
75. to restrict
76. index
77. tutor
78. forbidden
79. random
80. noticeable
81. apparent
82. considerable
83. to recommend
84. to expire
85. to interchange
86. resident
87. to stimulate
88. extensive
89. symbol
90. irresistible
91. compulsory
92. voluntary
93. volume
94. layman
95. uncommon
96. neutral
97. principle
98. reform

99. to confirm

100. to absorb

2. Test Two: Grammar

1. b	2. c	3. a	4. d	5. b
6. a	7. c	8. d	9. b	10. c
11. a	12. d	13. b	14. a	15. c
16. d	17. b	18. c	19. c	20. c
21. d	22. b	23. c	24. b	25. d
26. d	27. d	28. b	29. c	30. a
31. b	32. d	33. d	34. d	35. c
36. b	37. b	38. c	39. b	40. b
41. b	42. c	43. b	44. a	45. b
46. c	47. a	48. d	49. b	50. b
51. b	52. d	53. d	54. d	55. a
56. d	57. d	58. c	59. a	60. d
61. c	62. d	63. a	64. a	65. c
66. a	67. a	68. a	69. a	70. c
71. b	72. c	73. d	74. b	75. c
76. a	77. c	78. b	79. a	80. b
81. c	82. d	83. c	84. a	85. c
86. d	87. a	88. d	89. c	90. a
91. c	92. d	93. a	94. a	95. d
96. a	97. b	98. a	99. d	100. a

3. Test Three: Sentence Construction

1. A student who has studied English for a few years may have a vocabulary of thousands of words.

2. Between formal and colloquial English there is unmarked English, which is neither so literary and serious as formal English, nor so casual and free as colloquial English.

3. He bought a jeep in spite of his friend advising him against it.

4. Though good writing requires general and abstract words as well as specific and concrete ones, it is the latter that make writing vivid, real and clear.

5. It was raining so hard that they could not work in the fields.

6. The politician is concerned with successful elections, whereas the states-

man is interested in the future of his people.

7. Although the results of the experiment were successful, the school refused to give any help.

8. He chose to study computer science because of the good employment prospects.

9. If Mary hadn't walked so slowly she would have caught the train.

10. In the event of his not coming, the meeting will be put off till next week.

11. I said yes yesterday, but on second thoughts I must say no.

12. A cautious driver always brings with him a spare tyre in case he has a puncture.

13. There is plenty of food in the world. However, many people do not have enough to eat.

14. Although nuclear power can be used to make electricity, many people are against using nuclear power.

15. All the oil in the world will soon be used up, but we are not trying hard enough to find new sources of energy.

16. Agriculture is important to man because without agriculture we could not feed ourselves.

17. I'm not a member of the Church of England myself, therefore it would be rather impertinent of me to express an opinion.

18. Computer chess games are still a bit expensive, but they are getting cheaper all the time. Furthermore the chess-playing strength is rising.

19. After the cream is separated from the milk, it is made into butter.

20. The population of some Asian countries is increasing rapidly. For example, the population of Nepal will double in the next 25 years.

21. Western Europe has large reserves of fuel. For instance, the UK has a 250 year supply of coal.

22. A duck has webbed feet so that it can swim easily and walk on soft ground.

23. Rail travel is safer than road travel, because far fewer people are killed or injured during train travel.

24. The heated air expands and rises. As a result, an area of low pressure forms over the land.

25. Canada is similar to the United States in that the majority of its people speak English.

26. Governments will most probably not relocate entire cities just because they are in earthquake zones.

27. There were no economy seats available, so they were forced to buy expen-

sive ones.

28. Two experiments were conducted so that the hypothesis could be tested.

29. Middle-class families tend to have person-centred structures, whereas working-class families are usually positional.
(Working-class families are usually positional, whereas middel-class families tend to have person-centred structures.)

30. Middle-class children do well in most education systems. Working- class children, on the other hand, do relatively poorly.

31. Lima, La Paz (Bolivia) and Lisbon are all capitals. Los Angeles, however, is not.

32. Mauritius, Iceland and Sri Lanka consist of one main island, while New Zealand is formed by two.

33. Whales, dolphins, kangaroos and man are warm-blooded. Snakes, on the other hand, are not.

34. The environmental component of intelligence differs from whatever is due to heredity in that it is susceptible of manipulation.

35. The suffixes -er and -or mean "a person who", whereas -fy and -ize signify "to make".

36. The flight is an exhausting one. However, most of the birds arrive safely.

37. The warm climate makes the country attractive for tourists. In addition, hotels and food are cheap.

38. Eggs are cheap. Moreover, they are rich in protein.

39. Smith disagrees with some of Brown's conclusions, however he accepts his theory.

40. Socioeconomic status has been shown to relate to attitudes to education. Additionally, it is a predictor of academic attainment.

41. Cows' principal source of food is grass. Lions, by way of contrast, are carnivores.

42. She liked the people. Furthermore, she could identify with them.

43. The government's term of office was considered highly successful, while its education policy was occasionally problematic.

44. Despite the fact that its sales have declined in recent years, the company continues to hold a major share of the market.

45. In spite of the fact that there was a temporary recession in the early part of 1974, the decade was one of rapid economic growth.

46. The study has been widely acclaimed. Nevertheless, a few criticisms have been made of the implications drawn by the researchers.

47. The steel frames are covered with reinforced plastic film that is resistant to weather.

48. The plants are fed by inorganic nutrients dissolved in water which is supplied by a plastic pipeline.

49. When it is exposed to iodine vapour, the debris becomes ideal nuclei for the formation of ice crystals.
(The debris becomes ideal nuclei for the formation of ice crystals when it is exposed to iodine vapour.)

50. Letters and packets are taken to the sorting office, where the bags are emptied and letters separated from the packets.

Part Three: Common Writing Techniques in Testing
（第三部分：常用测试写作手法）

1. Narration （记叙文）

Exercise 1

Group one:	f g d c b a e
Group two:	a b f c e d h g i
Group three:	a c f b e d g

2. Comparison and Contrast （比较与对比）

Exercise 2

1. Sample Writing:

Ballet Dancers and Football Players

Both Ballet dancers and football players have a lot of things in common. However, there are also some differences between them.

Ballet dancers and football players differ in physical size and appearance. Yet both are highly trained athletes. Classical ballet and pro football both demand years of training, great strength, and agility. It takes endurance and speed to run for a touchdown. Likewise, these same qualities are used by a ballerina performing a series of turns in Swan Lake. As the football player practises plays, the dancer rehearses steps.

Physical skills, however, are used quite differently on a ballet stage than on a football field. Football players must react quickly to moves by their opponents. Ballet dancers, in contrast, follow precise steps designed by choreographers. Planned movements do not change during a ballet the way plays change during a football game. While football players use strength to overpower opponents, dancers express emotions or tell a story by using graceful movements.

To sum up, although ballet dancers and football players are similar in some ways, there are also some differences between them.

Exercise 3

1. Sample Writing:

The Flow of Electricity and Water

The flow of electricity through wires and cables from the main supply can be compared with the flow of water through pipes from a water tank.

When the tap is turned off, the water does not move, but when a tap is turned on, the height of the water in the tank exerts pressure on the water in the pipes and forces it through the outlet, i.e. the tap. This water pressure is comparable with voltage in electricity. The rate of the water flow, similar to the flow of current, is controlled by two things: the pressure and the size of the outlet. For example, a very narrow spray allows less water to flow than a wide pipe. Similarly in electricity, a very thin wire restricts or resists the flow of current. Electricians measure this resistance in ohms and the flow of the current in amperes (amps).

These are the common elements between the flow of electricity and water.

2. Sample Writing:

The Differences Between the Northern and Southern Polar Regions

The northern and southern polar regions are different in many ways. The most important difference concerns the distribution of land and water.

The northern Arctic regions are ice-covered sea, almost completely surrounded by land. The pole itself is in deep water. In the south, the Antarctica is a huge continent which is surrounded by a green ocean.

Because of this basic difference, other differences occur. The Arctic has a varied climate, while the Antarctic climate varies little; the Arctic has much plant life but the Antarctic is an empty desert.

And whereas the Arctic has been exploited economically for centuries, trade has never really touched the Antarctica.

These are the basic differences between the northern and southern polar regions.

Exercise 4

(1) Sample Writing for Topic 1:

Death penalty is a question of controversy. People have different notions about the matter: some uphold it as necessary; others condemn it as "murder by the state". Therefore, I would like to have a look at the question in this essay to decide how justifiable death penalty could be.

(*for*) One of the strong points of death penalty is that it is a necessary measure to maintain social order. In other words, social civilization is based on a well-formed system which stipulates that there are things we, as members of a society, can do, and things we are not supposed to do, such as deliberate murder. If one violates the system, then he/she has to pay for it — sometimes to forfeit his/her own life. Moreover, though most people find it difficult to accept the fact that a state should execute a murderer, it is virtually fair enough if we look at the matter from the point of view of the victim and his/her family. In fact, it is equally difficult for the family to accept the fact that their relatives died for something which should not have happened at all. That is to say death penalty is a way to guarantee social order and punish those who fail to comply with the law.

(*against*) The opponents of death penalty believe that the taking of a guilty person's life is just as violent as the killing of an innocent. In short, death penalty is too inhumane an act to have any place in a civilized society. For example, in China some people feel that putting a murderer to death will not bring the victim back to life again. Though their feeling is understandable in a sense, we really cannot let our feeling make a judgement on a matter of life and death. If that happened, we would impossibly maintain justice in our society and consequently civilization would be undermined.

In conclusion, I would like to say that it is extremely necessary and crucial to maintain death penalty in our society. Without it, it is hard to keep our civilization complete. However, I do believe that death penalty should be carefully handled. Each case should be thoro⁓ hly reviewed and concluded on the basis of facts. Only in this way can the pu   f death penalty be fulfilled and justice maintained.

(2) Sample Writing for   ⌐pic 2:

Many find it advantageous to purchase a home, but others find renting more suited to their needs. While there are advantages for both options, which one would be better for young foreign students?

Owning a home provides a number of benefits. For example, a homeowner can make more noise than someone who lives in an apartment without having to worry that every small noise might disturb neighbours. Owning is also an advantage because real estate generally appreciates in value over the years.

There are also benefits to renting. A renter is tied down only by the terms of the rental agreement or lease. If a renter wants to move, it is not necessary to find a buyer. In addition, a renter does not have to provide a large down payment as does a homeowner.

208

A foreign student who plans to return home after college or who wishes to transfer to another school often cannot be tied down to a house. The foreign student often does not have enough money for a down payment to purchase a home. Consequently, renting is the answer for most young foreign students.

Exercise 5

(1) Sample Writing:

Concentration of Smoke

The table shows the concentration of smoke in different parts of Britain in two different periods 1969~70 and 1971~72.

As can be seen in the table, the Smoke Control Act succeeded in reducing smoke pollution considerably in a short period. The table shows that in the industrial areas of Britain smoke concentrations were comparatively lower in 1971~72 than in 1969~70. For example, in Scotland there was a 44% micrograms per cubic metre in smoke concentration, in the north of England 80%, in the northwest 70%, and the West Midlands 48%.

In a less industrial area, such as southwest, the reduction was less—1%. The figures for 1971~72 are only 1 lower than those for 1969~70.

Wales is the only exception to the above trend. The figures for 1971~72 are 5% more than that for 1969~70.

(2) Sample Writing:

Sweden's Population

According to the graphs, Sweden's population in 1978 was very different from its population in 1751, before it became an industrialized nation.

In 1978, 16% of the population was over the age of 65, while only 13% were under the age of 10. The figures are presented in five-year blocks, and if one looks at these, the data is very interesting. The largest single group was the 30 to 35-year-olds, who made up 8% of the population, while the 0 to 4-year-olds only made up about 6%. About 6% of the population was over the age of 70, and of these there were twice as many women as men. This ratio of aged women to aged men is about the only similarity with the population structure of pre-industrial Sweden.

In 1751, there was only a third as many people alive over 65 (5%), whereas there were over twice as many people under the age of 10 (28%). In fact the largest single age group was the 0 to 4-year-olds, who made up 14% of the population. There were far fewer people over the age of 70: a sixth, in fact (1%).

Overall, it seems that Sweden in the 1970s had many more old people and far fewer children than pre-industrialized Sweden.

(3) Sample Writing:

The Spending on Defence

The two graphs depict the same thing seen in two different ways. Both show the spending on defence by the US government between 1956 and 1975.

The first diagram simply records the amount of money spent, in billions of dollars, during this period. The trend is almost uniformly upward from about $ 37 billion in 1956 to around $ 85 billion in 1975. The graph rises more steeply between 1965 and 1969, the period which corresponds with increasing military activity by the US in Vietnam.

The second graph throws a new light on the situation. This expresses defence spending as a percentage of GNP, thus relating one factor in the economy to the progress of the economy as a whole. It reveals that with the exception of the 1965-1969 period the rise in the amount of money spent on defence was matched by a fall in its value proportionate to the GNP. It declined from a figure of 9.6% in 1956 to under 6% in 1975.

3. Cause and Effect （原因与结果）

Exercise 1
 (1) cause: her slender diet
     effect: long life
 (2) cause: the extreme cold
     effects: the ice to freeze; glaciers to form
 (3) causes: overeating; the flu
     effect: stomachache
 (4) cause: too much sun
     effects: headache; sunburn
 (5) cause: depression
     effect: overate
 (6) effect: the war started
     cause: the desperate economic situation
 (7) cause: carried plenty of water
     effect: weren't thirsty
 (8) effect: Pulmonary lesions

	cause:	the human form of the tubercle bacillus
(9)	effect:	missed his flight
	cause:	a traffic hold-up
(10)	effect:	drunkenness
	cause:	too much alcohol
(11)	effect:	soil erosion
	causes:	heavy rain; strong winds
(12)	effect:	drought
	cause:	lack of rain
(13)	cause:	drought
	effect:	crops were ruined
(14)	cause:	cigarette smoking
	effect:	lung cancer
(15)	cause:	late for class
	effect:	got a tardy slip
(16)	cause:	held up by the snowstorm
	effect:	delay
(17)	cause:	the land absorbs heat from the sun
	effect:	the air above it becomes hot
(18)	cause:	out of health
	effect:	could not go to school
(19)	cause:	the computer has become smaller and cheaper
	effect:	more available to a greater number of people
(20)	cause:	the heated air expands; the heated air rises
	effect:	an area of low pressure forms over the land

Exercise 2

1. (1) d　　(2) c　　(3) b　　(4) a　　(5) h　　(6) g　　(7) f
   (8) e　　(9) l　　(10) k　　(11) j　　(12) i　　(13) o　　(14) n
   (15) m

Exercise 3

Sample Writing:

The World Climate

For the last hundred years the climate has been growing much warmer. This has had a number of different effects. Since the beginning of the 20th century, glaciers have been melting very rapidly. For example, the Muir Glacier in Alaska has retreated 2 miles in 10 years. Secondly, rising temperatures have been causing the snowline to retreat on mountains all over the world. In Peru, for example, it has retreated as much as 2700 feet in 60 years.

As a result of this, vegetation has also been changing. In Canada, the agricultural cropline has shifted 50 to 100 miles northward. In the same way cool-climate trees like birches and spruce have been dying over large areas of Eastern Canada. In Sweden the treeline has moved up the mountains by as much as 65 feet since 1930.

The distribution of wildlife has also been affected, many European animals moving northwards into Scandinavia. Since 1918, 25 new species of birds have been seen in Greenland, and in the United States birds have moved their nests to the north.

Finally, the sea has been rising at a rapidly increasing rate, largely due, as was mentioned above, to the melting of glaciers. In the last 18 years it has risen by about 6 inches, which is about four times the average rate of rise over the last 9,000 years.

Exercise 5
Paragraph 1:

The decision to keep a pet.... (a major change in a family's lifestyle)... pets require attention ... (family members have to be willing to give up some of their free time to care for them)... Pets depend on people to keep them clean, well fed, and healthy.... (families must arrange to have someone care for the animal when they go away on vacation)... Pets are fun but helpless... (are a big responsibility to a family)

Paragraph 2.

... some people in certain parts of the world thought cats were evil... (cats were feared and persecuted) (the population of rats and mice grew in the cities)... there were not enough cats to hunt them (cats are sometimes kept) ... they hunt mice ... they are good company.

Exercise 6
1. Sample Writing:

Why the Wind Blows from the Sea to the Land during the Day

During the day, the air above the land becomes hot because the land absorbs heat from the sun. The air above the land becomes hot, consequently the heated air expands and rises. It is like gases expanding when they are heated. As a result, an area of low pressure forms over the land.

The air over the sea is cold since the sea can not absorb heat as much as the land can. Over the sea is the high pressure area. Cold air from the high pressure area over the sea flows to the land, because the air flows from the high pressure area to low pressure area. This is why the wind blows from the sea to the land during the day.

2. Sample Writing:

Why Some Plants Become Sickly or Die

There are a variety of factors to be taken into consideration when analysing why some plants become sickly or die.

Dryness in the soil causes the leaves to lose freshness, or wilt, and may result in death of the plant.

On the other hand, too much water may result in the leaves losing their strength and drooping, or in their becoming yellow, and occasionally in the rotting of the leaves and stems.

While sunshine is necessary for plants, if it is too strong, the soil may be baked and the roots killed.

However, if there is no light, the leaves will become pale and the stems thin, and if not corrected, the consequence will be the death of the plant.

4. Description （描述）

Exercise 1
1. Sample Writing:

A Dry Battery

The dry form of the battery, which has an electromotive force of 1.5V, is the primary battery most commonly used today.

The positive pole consists of a carbon rod surrounded by a mixture of carbon powder and manganese dioxide. This mixture acts as the depolariser, i.e. a mixture of substances that prevent polarisation and the consequential reduction in potential difference. At the top of the carbon rod is a brass cap, which acts as the positive terminal. The carbon rod and the mixture of carbon powder and manganese dioxide, which are contained in a porous gauze bag, are placed in a zinc container, and the space between the bag and the container is filled with the electrolyte, which consists of a paste of ammonium chloride and zinc chloride. The zinc container acts as the negative pole. The top of the battery is closed with a sealing compound.

2. Sample Writing:

A Spray Aerosol Container

A spray aerosol container can be divided into five main parts. In the middle of it, there is a curved tube, which is connected to the spraying nozzle. On the left of the tube, the upper part contains vapour, while the lower contains a liquid product and liquified propellant. On the right side of the tube, on the other hand, the upper part contains propellant gas, while the lower is a vapourisation.

3. Sample Writing:

An Electric Motor

An electric motor is a machine for converting electrical energy into mechanical energy. A motor can be designed to run on direct or alternating current. Its most important parts are the rotor, the stator and the brushgear.

The rotor is the moving part. It contains an armature, which is a set of wire loops wound on a steel core. The armature and core are mounted on a shaft which runs on bearings. It provides a means of transmitting power from the motor.

The rotor also contains a commutator. This consists of a number of copper segments insulated.

Exercise 2
1. Sample Writing:

How to Develop a Film

After all the photographs on a film have been taken, the reel or cassette is removed from the camera to be processed.

First, the film itself must be stripped from its backing paper in complete darkness. It is then immediately loaded into a developing tank, in a spiral to avoid contact between its surfaces. The tank is tightly closed to keep out light.

Next, the tank is filled with developer, which is a dilute solution of hydroquinone and sodium sulphite and other chemicals. A thermometer is needed as the developing time depends on the temperature as well as on the strength of the solution. The film is turned round from time to time in the developing tank, or the tank is inverted and the developer must be poured off at the right moment, to avoid over or under-developing. Some developers can be reused.

The developed film, which has light and dark parts, must now be washed in a 2% solution of acetic acid to remove all the developer. It is then treated with fixing solution to remove any undeveloped silver bromide. Before the film is removed from the developing tank to dry, it is washed in running water. The negatives, when thoroughly dry, are now finally ready for printing.

2.. Sample Writing:

How to Mend a Flat Bicycle Tyre

Flat tyres are often caused by punctures which leak air with varying degrees of speed. Punctures which are not huge holes can be repaired. You'll need a tube patch kit containing patches, glue, an abrasive surface e.g. sandpaper, tyre irons and chalk.

You should begin by deflating the tyre. But first of all, it'd be a good idea to check if the flat tyre is just due to a faulty valve. You can do this by placing a drop of spit or water on the end of the valve stem. A leaky valve will bubble or spit back. In this case, just tighten the valve. However, if there is no fault in the valve, you should begin, as mentioned before, by deflating the tyre. Then you should work the tyre back and forth with your hands to get the edge of the tyre free of the rim. If this doesn't work, use the tyre irons as levers to free the tyre. When the edge is off the rim, you should push the valve stem up into the tyre, and re-move the tube. At this stage you should inflate the tube and rotate it past your ear. If you can find the puncture through the hiss of escaping air, it's a good idea to mark the spot with chalk. If you can't, then you should place all of the tube in wa-ter, look for escaping air bubbles, and then mark the spot with the chalk.

You can use the sandpaper to rub the spot rough enough and then apply glue to the spot. You will wait for two or three minutes. When the glue is dry enough, you take out a piece of patch and put it right on the spot, then press it hard. This is the whole process of mending a flat tyre.

3. Sample Writing:

How to Make Paper

Modern paper is manufactured from a mixture of various fibres like rags, linen, wood, waste paper. The main ingredient is of course wood pulp, produced from complete trees after the bark has been removed. The main areas of production are Finland and Canada, where the trees are cut down, taken to the saw mill, and chopped up. The pieces of wood are then ground up and mixed with other substances, such as glue, to make a paper fibre mixture, and then poured out onto wire screens. These are large areas of wire mesh — sheets of metal with a large number of holes in them. Here the water is extracted from the mixture, which is dried and passed through many rollers to press it into shape. This process produces one continuous sheet of paper, which is wound into a large roll at the end of the manufacturing process.

Exercise 3

1. Sample Writing:

How a Camera Works

A camera is basically a simple instrument. Its name comes from its most important part, the camera obscura (Latin for dark chamber). Photographs are produced when rays of light enter this chamber through a small opening (the aperture), and strike against a sensitive film. The aperture contains a convex lens which refracts the light. The surface of the film is covered with silver bromide emulsion. This captures the image which is brought in by the rays of light. The aperture is closed or opened by a shutter, which is the only moving part in a simple camera. This is mounted behind the lens. It is, of course, usually closed. In more refined cameras, the speed of the shutter and size of the aperture can be adjusted, to vary the length of an exposure and the quantity of light to be allowed in. Shorter exposures are needed to photograph moving objects, and a wider aperture lets in more light on a dull day.

2. Sample Writing:

How a Refrigerator Works

A refrigerator is really nothing more than a box in which articles can be kept at a cool temperature. The temperature inside the box is regulated by means of a thermostat. Apart from the thermostat, the refrigerator mechanism includes a motor-driven compressor, a condenser and a set of thin, metal evaporator coils, into which is pumped a liquid refrigerant called Freon.

When a liquid evaporates it absorbs heat. The refrigerant used in a refrigerator has a very low boiling point and it evaporates in the metal coils. As this happens it absorbs heat and as a result, the evaporator coils cool down.

As soon as the temperature inside the refrigerator rises above a predetermined level, the thermostat causes the motor to start. Freon vapour is drawn from the evaporator coils by the compressor, reducing the pressure and allowing liquid refrigerant to move into them. This liquid in its turn evaporates, absorbing heat and cooling the refrigerator. The cool refrigerant passes through the condenser, where it is changed back into a liquid form and is eventually forced back into the evaporator coils.

The process continues until a pre-set temperature is reached. At this point the thermostat cuts out the compressor and the refrigerator remains idle. When the temperature rises above the pre-determined level, the thermostat triggers the compressor into action once more and the cooling cycle recommences.

Exercise 4

1. Sample Writing:

The Life-Cycle of Schistosome

The life-cycle of schistosome can be divided into two main stages.

The first stage takes place in the water. When the eggs hatch, the embryoes enter the bodies of water snails. They develop into worms inside the snails. Eventually the worms return to the water.

The second stage takes place in the water, too. The worms penetrate the skin of any person who happens to be standing in the water. Once inside the human body they move through the blood vessels to the liver. They remain in the liver until they are adults, and then move to the bladder, where they lay their eggs, causing severe inflammation. Finally, the eggs are excreted into the water. At this stage the life cycle of schistosome begins all over again.

5. Argument （议论文）

Exercise 1

1. (1) opinion   (2) fact   (3) fact   (4) fact
   (5) opinion   (6) opinion   (7) fact   (8) opinion
   (9) opinion   (10) opinion   (11) fact   (12) opinion
2. (1) fact   (2) fact   (3) fact   (4) opinion   (5) opinion   (6) opinion
3. (1) opinion   (2) fact   (3) fact   (4) mixed   (5) mixed
   (6) fact   (7) opinion   (8) opinion   (9) opinion   (10) fact

Exercise 2

1. Paragraph 1. The jury system promotes injustice.
   Paragraph 2. Capital punishment is needed for the protection of the community.

Paragraph 3. Capital punishment is a procedure unworthy of any civilized nation.

Paragraph 4. School athletes should participate in school sports but should not be excused from taking a full schedule of other subjects.

Exercise 4

(1) ... For example, there are the difficulties associated with parking; there is the loss of time caused by traffic congestion; and there is a resulting decline in the numbers of people using public transport.

(2) ... For example, men are very much stronger physically than women, and as a consequence can carry greater weights, run faster, and make longer sustained efforts. Men, too, do not become emotionally involved in a situation as women do; as a result, they are less prejudiced and do not make biased decisions. This gives them the advantage of being able to assess situations objectively, to see what is required and do it.

(3) ... For example, a homeowner can make more noise than someone who lives in an apartment without having to worry that every small noise might disturb neighbours.

(4) ... In the United States, for example, the South is the part of the country where the people smile most frequently. In New England they smile less, and in the western part of New York State still less.

(5) ... A new study in the US has found that leukaemia, for example, appears seven times more often among people who have spent their lives with smokers. Cancers of the cervix and breast were also strongly linked with "passive smoking".

Exercise 7

2.

Passage 1: (1) First (2) Second (3) On the other hand (4) Next
(5) since

Passage 2: (1) In addition (2) Furthermore (3) Besides (4) for
(5) Finally (6) Therefore

Exercise 8

(1) d b e c f a h g
(2) g c f b e a d
(3) e f a g b h c i d

218

Part Four: Testing Skills
（第四部分：测试技巧）

1. Analysing the Task （审题）

Exercise 1
    (1) ... (capital punishment)
    (2) ... (a college education and a degree) ... (college degree) ...
    (3) ... (the wind)...
    (4) ... (components of hot water system)...
    (5) ... (the potential benefits) ... (of continuing education)...
    (6) ... (pure water) ...
    (7) ... (technological development) ...
    (8) ... (scientific research in your particular field)
    (9) ... (the test of English) ...
  (10) ... (the use of animals in scientific laboratory tests) ...

Exercise 2
    (1) What are the stages involved ...
    (2) (Is it necessary? Why?)
    (3) (Should it be permitted? Why?)
    (4) (Which effort is better? Why?)
    (5) What ... would you offer ...
    (6) To what extent has... changed over the past 15 years?
    (7) In what circumstance can ... be justified?
    (8) (What are the most important adjustments to learning and writing styles for overseas students?)
    (9) (What is the precess like? What equipment is needed?)
  (10) (What are the effects? What are the methods?)

Exercise 3
    (1) a sponsoring agency
    (2) a course teacher
    (3) a university teacher

Exercise 4

(1) Topic: the wind

Question: Why does it blow from the sea to the land?

Audience: a teacher

Task requirements:

- a. Time: no more than 15 minutes.
- b. Task type: description
- c. Information sources: the diagram and your own knowledge and experience.
- d. Writing requirements: relevant to the question and well organized.
- e. Length: at least 100 words.

(2) Topic: smoking

Question: What are the effects of smoking and methods of risk reduction?

Audience: your tutor

Task requirements:

- a. Time: no more than 15 minutes.
- b. Task type: description
- c. Information sources: from the diagram and your own knowledge and experience.
- d. Writing requirements: three or four paragraphs relevant to the question and well organized.
- e. Length: at least 100 words.

(3) Topic: the use of computers in language teaching activities.

Question: What happened?

Audience: a university teacher

Task requirements:

- a. Time: no more than 30 minutes.
- b. Task type: a report
- c. Information sources: your own knowledge and experience.
- d. Writing requirements: The essay is well organized. Your point of view is clearly expressed and your argument is supported by relevant information.
- e. Length: at least 150 words.

(4) Topic: the use of animals in scientific laboratory tests

Question: Is it justified?

Audience: a course teacher

Task requirements:

a. Time: no more that 30 minutes.

b. Task type: an argument

c. Information sources: your own knowledge and experience.

d. Writing requirements: The essay is well organized. Your point of view is clearly expressed and your argument is supported by relevant information .

e. Length: at least 150 words.

4. Writing the Body （写正文）

Exercise 2

（1） ... of our system of preferential voting. In simple terms it is a process of eliminating the candidates one by one until there is only one candidate left. This candidate may not have been the first choice of all the voters, but he or she is the one preferred by most of the voters after all the others have been eliminated. In first-past-the-post voting systems, a voter has only one vote and a candidate can be elected with only a minority of the votes. But in the preferential system, voters get two or more votes. If their first choice is not elected, they have a second choice.

（2） ... staying single gives you the freedom to spend your own money in your own way. And you can enjoy the amount of free time in any way you prefer.

（3） ... the horse cannot seek its own food and water, people must supply these necessities. Owners must see that a horse gets enough exercise. Owners and trainers value a horse's health. With care and good treatment by humans, a horse will live a long, healthy life.

（4） ... it is not only central but also the heart of London's entertainment world. Within a few hundred yards of it we find most of London's best-known theatres and cinemas, the most famous restaurants and the most luxurious night-clubs.

（5） ... the average Englishman is keen on working with his hands and partly because he feels, for one reason or another, that he must do for himself many household jobs for which, some years ago, he would have hired professional help. The main reason for this is a financial one: the high cost of labour has meant that building and decorating costs have reached a level which makes them prohibitive for house-proud English people of modest means. So, if they wish to keep their houses looking bright and

smart, they have to tackle some of the repairing and decorating themselves.

Exercise 3

(1) ... two factors usually considered in determining the basic wage, from
which most other awards are calculated, are the ability of industry to pay
and the needs of the workers.

(2) ... since the law made it easier to get a divorce, the number of divorces
has increased. In fact one marriage in every three now ends in divorce.

(3) ... we all smile to show friendliness no matter what country we come
from. Everywhere it is customary to exchange gifts, or presents, on special occasions.

(4) ... the "lead" of a pencil is made of carbon, coal is made of carbon, and
so are diamonds. A number of other things such as wood, plants, and oil
are made very largely of carbon, but have other substances as well. The
molecules which make up our bodies depend on carbon.

(5) ... some instruments are played by blowing air into them. These are
called wind instruments. In some of these the air is made to vibrate inside
a wooden tube, and these are said to be of the woodwind family. Examples of woodwind instruments are the flute, the clarinet and the bassoon.

(6) ... it can be the result of windblown dust, smoke from bushfires, salt
particles from the oceans, gases from the decay of plant and animal life,
and occasional torrents of gases and dust particles from volcanic eruptions.

(7) ... about one million people have a drinking problem; 10 million working
days are lost each year through alcohol-induced absenteeism; half of all violent crimes are committed by people who have been drinking; a third of
the drivers killed in car accidents are over the legal alcohol limit. The social costs of alcohol abuse in Britain probably amount to over 2 million
pounds a year.

(8) ... used hot springs for baths. More recently, it has been used to heat
buildings such as greenhouses, and to generate electricity.

Exercise 4

(1) First; Then; Then
(2) To begin with; therefore; Moreover; Furthermore; In addition
(3) On the one hand; On the other hand
(4) As a result; because; Consequently
(5) At the first stage;

222

At the second stage;

At the third stage;

At the last stage

5．Writing a Conclusion （写结尾）

Exercise 1

(1) (Concluding Paragraph)

On the whole, it is useless to point out that we really cannot get more teachers, more schools and more equipment. In this world we need more educated people. If we are to survive in this scientific age, we must be educated to live in and protect our country. I say it is a matter of national importance to raise the leaving age immediately.

(2) (Concluding Paragraph)

In brief, the regulations mentioned above are very important and failure to observe these regulations places all passengers at risk.

(3) (Concluding Paragraph)

In a word, we should get into the good habit of saving time and make our time valuable.

(4) (Concluding Paragraph)

At this point, the student has completed these two required documents and may then enrol.

(5) (Concluding Paragraph)

In conclusion, all children in schools should wear uniforms and with these school uniforms on they are still free individuals.

6．Checking the Writing （检查写作）

Exercise 1

1．(1) abandoned; children

(2) stopped; abruptly

(3) accommodation; thousand

(4) vacation; accumulated

(5) accelerate; recovery

(6) almost; alert

(7) ambiguous; impossible; assignment

(8) assume; arrived

(9) behaviour; because

(10) bitter; sugar

(11) cancelled

(12) colleague

(13) receives; compliments

(14) confident; passed

(15) congestion; difficult

(16) dilemma; whether

(17) doubtful; contract

(18) duration; examination

(19) vitamins; energy

(20) essential

(21) efforts; futile

(22) implied

(23) inhabit

(24) innovations; century

(25) inspected; annually

(26) invariable; necessary

(27) penetrated

(28) permanently

(29) postponed

(30) routine; excellent

2. (1) common; experience; animals; natural; sensibly

   (2) particular; wrong; circumstances; Western; basic

   (3) ancient; associations; eventually; international; official

   (4) suggestion; television; definite; value; allowed

   (5) assumption; community; individuals; increasing; attendance

   (6) commonly; essential; justice; widespread; unsatisfactory

3. Passage 1: processes; collection; rubber; before; remaining; ready

   Passage 2: attempt; convince; government; celebrate; seen; accelerating; disappearance; doubt; compelled

Exercise 2

Passage 1: ... is an instrument ...

... microscope consists of a ...

... platform contains a number of ...

... The latter is used to control ...

... is good enough for ordinary laboratory ...

.... electron microscope is used.

Passage 2: ... teaching is so frequently under attack ...

... some justification is needed to retain it. ...

... students have no opportunity to ask questions ...

... lectures which consist in part of the contents of ...

... Medical and dental students who have reported on teaching ...

Part Five: Sample Tests
（第五部分：模拟试题）

Sample Test Five （模拟试题五）

Writing Task 1:

Describe a camera, and explain how it works.

Sample Writing 1: (Score: 8)

The purpose of a camera is to take photographs, to have a permanent record on film of a scene, a friend's face or whatever. When a light-sensitive film is exposed to light for a certain period of time, an image can be recorded on the film.

At the front of the camera is a glass lens which projects or throws the image onto a film which is stretched out at the back of the camera. On the top, there is a shutter release button. The shutter will let in only the correct amount of light. There are five positions of the aperture settings on the top of the camera, marked by the sun or cloud signs. At the back of the camera there is a piece of glass called the viewfinder which *links* to a sort of small glass window at the front. The film window will tell the number of pictures taken. The handle to wind film is just underneath the film window.

When you want to take a photograph, you must follow these simple instructions. First, take the film cassette out of its packet, and insert it into the back of the camera. Wind the film on until *a* number "1" appears in the film window at the back of the camera. Now set the aperture to one of the five positions according to the light conditions. Look through the viewfinder and move the camera until what you want to photograph appears between the white lines. Hold the camera steady and press the shutter release button slowly. That is all you have to do to get perfect pictures.

links: is linked

a: the

226

Sample Writing 2: (Score: 7)

The picture given shows an advanced camera. It can be used easily and conveniently.

The shape of the camera is a rectangle. The lens *are* in the front of the camera on the left while the viewfinder is on the right. On the top of the camera, there are shutter release button on the left and aperture settings in the centre. The latter will be set according to the weather conditions. The film window is on the back and beneath it is the handle to wind the film.

The camera works like this: Firstly, the film is fitted in and the number "1" is shown on the film window. Then the lens cover is opened and the aperture settings is fixed at a proper position. Next, the *pictures are* selected through the viewfinder. Finally, the shutter release button can be pressed after the picture wanted is chosen.

This is a simple description of an advanced camera and its process of working.

are: is

pictures are: picture is

Sample Writing 3: (Score: 6)

The picture below shows the camera's construction and how it works.

In the front of the camera, there are the lens with lens cover and front of the viewfinder. In its back, there are film window and back part of the viewfinder. On the top is the shutter release button and the aperture settings. And at the bottom, there is a handle to wind film.

It works as follows:

First of all, the cover of the film box is opened and the film is put into it. Then the cover is closed and the film is turned to the first *place through foberving the film window*. The next step is to find a suitable scene through the viewfinder and check it in the aperture settings. Finally, the shutter release button is put down and the picture is taken.

All the above description is the construction and process of a camera.

place through foberving the film window: picture

All the above: The above

Writing Task 2:

What are the advantages and/or disadvantages brought to your particular situation by computers?

Sample Writing 1: (Score: 8)

Computers have found its wide application in our daily life and industrial work. To my particular working condition, it also plays a more and more important role. There are, however, both advantages and disadvantages brought about by computers.

Firstly, one of the advantages of using *computer* is convenience. We can now store and take out files by using computers and no longer need to rewrite the same file again and again. It is especially convenient when we want to make a new file by slightly changing an original one.

The second advantage to be mentioned here is that computers make us work more efficiently. Huge amount of data processing can be done with the help of computers, which save us a lot of time. And if we use it properly, we can eventually get the results we want directly from what we put in through computers.

The last advantage I can list here at this moment is that the use of computers can minimize errors made by human subjectiveness. We usually make mistakes by judging *our* bias on objective results through making choices on original experimental data, because there are some situations in which we should not take everything into account. By using computers the choices can be made by computers objectively.

On the other hand there are some disadvantages induced by the use of computers in my work. First of all, it makes me lazy, for I do not analyse the process step by step, which is sometimes necessary. Secondly, computers can also make mistakes. For example, the *lost* of files can cause great difficulties in our work.

On the whole, computers have both advantages and disadvantages. But fairly speaking, everyone should admit that its advantages overweigh its disadvantages. We should make use of computers more and more in our work.

computer: a computer
our: with
lost: loss

228

Sample Writing 2: (Score: 7)

With the development of science and technology *computer* is used in many fields, such as industry, business, military and domestic life. Does the computer bring advantages to us?

The computer can do very complex work. According to a report of computer experts, some culculation which should take one year of time by 100 persons could be fulfilled in 10 hours by *compute*. So people can do many other things with the help of computers.

The computer provides the possibility to store information which could be found out very conveniently. For example, a company receives more than 100 files everyday. If these files are put in the office, *it* would occupy more and more space, on the other hand, people should spend more time to find the file he wants. But computers can store these files in harddisk and set up the index. So finding a file is very fast.

The computer also can be used in industry for controlling machines and in domestic life such as *shopping*, *booking* tickets.

To sum up, computer application is spreading almost every corner of the world. It brings more and more advantages to us. We should say the computer is one of the most important parts in our life.

    computer: the computer
    computer: a computer
    it: they
    shopping, booking: shopping and booking

Sample Writing 3: (Score: 6)

The computer is a morden high-technology. It is playing an *importantly* role in our society. It has brought us not only advantages but also disadvantages.

The application of computers has brought us enormous advantages in our *life*. Owing to its function of data processing, for example, it can help scientists *solve the more* complicated calculations. Moreover, it can help us do some repetitive and tedious work, such as payroll, long-term weather forcasting because of its efficient function of storing information. *What is important, the intellegient computer would be able to do some more sophisticated technical work for us.*

However, it can not be denied that the computer has given rise to many problems. With the advent of computers, many people have lost their jobs. In addition, the application of computers has made more and more people lazy and discontent, because the computer has replaced their routine work and chores.

By any means, although the computer has brought us some disadvantages, its advantages are uncomparable.

importantly: important
life: lives
solve the more: solve more
What is important, the intellegient computer would be able to do some more sophisiticated technical work for us: This sentence should be omitted here.

Sample Test Six （模拟试题六）

Writing Task 1:

Write a short paragraph describing the life-cycle of schistosome, the parasite causing bilharzia.

Sample Writing 1: (Score: 8)

The life cycle of schistosome can be divided into two stages. The first stage happens in the human bodies, and the second in the water snails.

When *the people are* in the water which *were* contaminated by worms, the worms penetrate the skin and enter the human body. Once inside the body, the worms pass through the blood vessels and move to the liver where they grow up to adults and increase in numbers. Meanwhile, the patients suffer from the bilharzia. Then the adults move to the bladder where they lay their eggs and cause bladder inflammation. After that they are excreted into the water. The next stage starts in the water. The eggs are hatched and become embryos and later enter the snails in which they change to young worms . Finally the worms leave the snails and pass into the water. Then the life cycle of schistosome begins again.

the people are: a person is
were: is

230

Sample Writing 2: (Score: 7)

Bilharzia is a disease that seriously *threaten* people's health and *life*. It is caused by the parasite called schistosome.

The picture shows the life-cycle of schistosome. First, the parasite exists in the water. By any chance they go into the snail where the worms change form. Then they leave the snail and pass into water. When man swims or *washes* in the water, the worms will enter the man's body, where they change and increase in number, and as a result bring about illness. Finally, the worms leave *man's body passing into water*.

We notice that the snail is an infection medium. To provent bilharzia we must wipe out snails.

threaten: threatens
life: lives
washes: stands
man's body passing into water: the man's body and pass into water

Sample Writing 3: (Score: 6)

The following writing *is description* of the life-cycle of schistosome, the parasite causing bilharzia.

The life-cycle of schistosome can *divide into* several stages. When the worms leave snails, they pass into water. When men work in the water, the worms enter men. In a man's body, the worms change and increase in number. At this stage, men develop bilharzia. Then the worms leave the man's body and pass into water again. In the water the worms enter snails. They change form in the snail's body and increase in number. The worms leave snails and pass into water again. The life-cycle of schistosome starts once again.

The above writing *is description* of the life-cycle of schistosome.

is description: is a description
divide into: be divided into
is description: is a description

Writing Task 2:

Should immunization be permitted in your country?

Sample Writing 1: (Score: 8)

Immunization is a method which uses vaccines to prevent certain diseases. Since immunization was permitted in our country several decades ago, the incidence of some diseases has been reduced apparently.

First of all, different organizations of immunization *had been* established in our country to carry out the immune programme.

Second, special workers have been trained. The State Health Organization provides the medical workers with opportunity to learn how to inject the vaccines and store them properly.

Third, knowledge of vaccination is given to all the people *by* TV and radio programmes, newspapers, etc. which enhances the realization to the importance of immunization.

Finally, the vaccination is implemented. In our country, the vaccines of tuberculosis and hepatitis-B are injected to newborn babies within 24 hours after birth. The vaccines of diphtheria, pertussis, tetanus and poliomyelitis are given within six months after birth. The measles is given at eighth months and two years old. In addition, we also use other vaccines to prevent children from epidemic diseases such as flu and encephalitis-B in the special period of the year.

had been: have been
by: through

Sample Writing 2: (Score: 7)

Due to the weather, the environment and physical conditions, people often suffer from various fatal diseases. As a result, a lot of people lose their lives and become disabled. Therefore, immunization is very necessary in our country.

It is indeed true that with the development of medical science in our country, health care *has a great improvement*, of course, including immunization. For example, children must accept measles precaution *periodly* since they are born. So, very few children suffer from measles which often cause children to become disabled. What is more, when some diseases prevail, such as hepatitis and flu, emergency preventive measures will be taken immediately for adults, particularly for children by injection and medicine. Thus, epidemic can be controlled quickly, and the rate of *death* decreased.

To sum up, the immunization should and must be allowed for the people's health in our country.

> has a great improvement: has been improved greatly
> periodly: periodically
> death: fatal diseases

Sample Writing 3: (Score: 6)

Should immunization be permitted in China? The answer is "Yes, it should". In fact, a long time ago *Chinese Government* signed a health care law which stipulates that children *must* take immunization after their birth.

Vaccine is one of the greatest inventions in the field of medical science because it has saved innumerable *people's life*. Long before, smallpox made people frightened since they could do nothing with the small virus. It is vaccine that protected people against the disease.

Nowadays, more and more vaccines are invented which result in *various diseases reducing*. But in some countries, especially in Africa, some diseases that could be prevented by injection of vaccines still threat people's lives and health. So immunization must be done quickly in these countries.

In China, immunization has made a great success. Many diseases which used to be very common disappeared. We get the benefits from immunization so we will develop it in the future.

> Chinese Government: the Chinese government
> must: should
> people's life: lives of the people
> various diseases reducing: the reduction of various diseases

Sample Test Seven （模拟试题七）

Writing Task 1:

As a course assignment you are asked to write a description of the changes in the popularity of cinema and television from 1957 to 1974.

Sample Writing 1: (Score: 8)

The graph below illustrates the dramatic changes in the popularity of cinema and television from 1957 to 1974.

In 1957, accoridng to the graph, cinema admission was nearly 870 million and television licence was only about 7 million. But after that the gradual changes happened. The last 17 years saw the steady growth of television licences and the sharp decline of cinema *admission*. By 1974, the number of cinema admissions had reached less than 100 million. But the number of television licences has increased to over 17.5 million. We can see from this that more and more people would like to stay at home watching TV rather than going out to see films.

In a word, this graph shows us that TV is more popular than cinema. And it also tells us the changes of attitude of people toward entertainment in their *life*.

admission: admissions
life: lives

Sample Writing 2: (Score: 7)

The graph shows the changes in the popularity of cinema and television from 1957 to 1974. The horizontal axis indicates time, and the vertical axis indicates *number of* admissions and licences.

As can be seen, the popularity of cinema greatly decreased between 1957 and 1974. In 1957, the number of cinema admissions was 700 million which decreased to 125 million in 1974.

On the other hand, the number of television licences increased since 1957. In 1957, the number of licences was only 7million which *raised* gradually since 1960. Towards 1974, the number of licences reached a peak of 17 million.

The trend shows that watching television has become more popular than seeing *cinema* during the period from 1957 to 1974.

number of: the number of
raised: had risen
cinema: films

Sample Writing 3: (Score: 6)

The following graph shows us the changes in the popularity of cinema and television from 1957 to 1974.

There *are* 900 million people who entered cinemas in 1957 in Great Britain. Since then the number of people who saw films dropped down and there was a sharp fall from 1957 to 1959, then the fall was slight, only about 125 million people went to cinemas in 1974.

On the other hand, the number of people who watched television increased from 1957 to 1974. There were 7 million licences in 1957, and there were 17.5 million licences in 1974 in the U. K. *The increasing of number of* licences was one reason why the number of admissions dropped.

This description above *just is* the changes in the popularity of cinema and television.

are: were
The increasing of number of: The increasing number of
just is: is just

Writing Task 2:

To what extent has women's social position changed over the past 20 years? What recommendations could you make to improve the current situation?

Sample Writing 3: (Score: 8)

The past two decades have seen great changes of women's social position in both the developed countries and developing countries. The scene in China is a good example which reflects the changes in the last 20 years.

Since the founding of the P. R. China in 1949, most of the women in China *were* liberated politically, economically and socially. Women enjoy equal rights to education, employment and political life. Women go out to work as men do. They have gained their social, economic and political independence in our society. Although great achievements have been made in women's social status, it must be pointed out that there is still *long way to go to* achieve true equity for women in the society. The discrimination against women in our society is the barrier which hinders women to have equal rights with men in education, employment and political life. According to a survey carried out by the educational authorities in China, girl students remain the largest population (over 80%) among the school drop-outs and nonattenders. This makes girls become illiterate when they grow up. In the labour market, it is more likely for the employers to hire men instead of women. Even though women are employed the payment is lower than men.

From what mentioned above, great efforts need to *make* to improve the education condition for girls. The law on compulsory education should be strictly enforced in every part of China. In order to ensure the equity to employment and payment, the law which protects women's legal rights should be effectively carried out in the society.

In a word, we admit that great changes happened have improved women's social status. And at the same time we have to notice that in order to achieve the goal of true equity for women in our society greater endeavours need to be made in the days to come.

were: have been
long way to go to: a long way to
make: be made

Sample Writing 2: (Score: 7)

It *is not denying* that women's social position has *increased* greatly in the past 20 years. However, in some aspects women's social position is still lower than men's. Therefore, it is necessary to discuss if women could share equal rights with men.

It is indeed true that women have won their own social position. They can go out to work and earn money in order to maintain their lives. Furthermore, some women even enter political affairs to manage important things, such as Sar Xian He in the UK, Wu Yi in China. At first sight, women share *right of equal promotion* in society with men.

However, it is also true that women haven't got equal treatment as men. For example, whether in China or in other countries, women do the same job as men, but they get lower salary. Furthermore, in most families, women do more housework than men. Concerning with women's physical conditions, it is not rational. Therefore, we can not say that women's social position has been improved in all aspects.

In conclusion, although women's social position has been changed during the past 20 years, there is still a lot of work to be done at present and in the future.

is not denying: can not be denied
increased: been improved
right of equal promotion: equal rights

Sample Writing 3: (Score: 6)

With the development of society women's social position *changed*, especially

236

in the past 20 years. Women *play important* role as men in society. But there is a difference of change between the developed countries and the developing countries.

In the developed countries, such as the United States and the United Kingdom, more and more women go to work. *It has* occupied 40% in the work force. With the increase of female employees the women's social position *rised*. But women do more domestic work than men. So women spend double time for work.

In the developing countries, women's employed population is similar to men's, but they have to spend more than 16 hours for the whole day's work. On the other hand, although women do the same work as men, their income is less than men's.

In order to improve women's situation, firstly, women should work part time in order to look after the family; secondly, women should do the work suitable *for female*, such as *food*, textile.

changed: has changed
play important: play an important
It has: women have
rised: has been raised
for female: for them owing to their physical conditions
food, : food processing and

Sample Test Eight (模拟试题八)

Writing Task 1:

A friend who lives abroad will shortly be visiting your university and has asked you to make arrangements for his stay. Write a letter informing him of what you have done.

Sample Writing 1: (Score: 8)

Dept. of Architecture
SW Jiaotong University
Chengdu
11/05/96

Mr. Smith

Dept. of Architecture
Cambridge University
Cambridge 1w J2
U.K.

Dear Mr. Smith,

I have received your letter dated April 5, 1996 in which you have asked me to make arrangements for your stay here. I am glad to tell you that all relevant things have been arranged as follows:

First of all, I will meet you at the airport when you arrive here. Then I will take you to our university *reception that* I have booked a room for you. On the second day of your arrival, you will be invited to attend our teaching activity in a small group. In the afternoon, I will take you to visit our students'design work of architecture. On the third day, I have arranged a lecture at which I hope you could give us an introduction to the teaching features of architecture at Cambridge. In the evening, I will have a small party for you at which you will have more chance to communicate with our students as well as our staff. On the last day I will see you off at the airport.

If there is anything inconvenient for you in this schedule, please let me know as soon as possible.

I am looking forward to your reply and wish you a pleasant journey.

Sincerely yours,
Qiu Gang

reception that: hotel in which

Sample Writing 2: (Score: 7)

P.O. Box 802
Chu Guo Bu
Beijing Language and Cul-
   ture University.
Beijing, 100083
China
10/05/96

Dear Jack,

I am very glad to hear that you are going to visit our university and I am very pleased to arrange for you to have a comfortable stay here.

No problem with accommodation and eating. You can live in our dormitory *where* one of our roommates will go back home and will not come back until you leave Beijing. And we can eat in *students'* dining hall.

I have booked a set of tour tickets according to your taste and preference. I hope you will like them.

The rest can be discussed when you come.

Make sure to phone me at 01-62017531 extension 2666 just before you leave home, and give me the information about your arrival. I will meet you at the airport.

Best wishes.

Yours sincerely,

Wang Li

where: since
students': the students'

Sample Writing 3: (Score: 6)

P.O. Box 805
Chu Guo Bu
Beijing Language and
    Culture University
Beijing, 100083
China
10th Aug. 1996

Dear Xin:

I am very pleased that you will visit our university *shortly*. I have made some arrangements for your stay here.

I will meet you at 9:30, 1st Sept. *at London Airport*, *nearby the information desk*. Then I will drive you to the apartment which I have rented for you. It is located near our university and has a very comfortable room and a wonderful view. I will hold a party on the following evening and invite several of our classmates who are in London now to welcome you.

I also have arranged for you to visit two famous places during your stay here, one of them is the Scottish Borders, the other is Glasgow.

I am looking forward to seeing you soon.

Best regards.

Yours sincerely,

Liu Ying

shortly: for a short time

at London Airport, nearby the information desk: near the information desk at London Airport

Writing Task 2:

You have read the "General Introduction" of a summer course. Write a report to your course supervisor. Explain briefly what course you want to take abroad and what qualifications you hope to get, and what you hope to do with these qualifications when you return to your own country.

Sample Writing 1: (Score: 8)

I am a Chinese student sponsored by the British Council and going to take the research attachment in the University of Edinburgh for one year. The programme will begin in this coming October. In order to make full use of the one year's time, I would like to registrate your summer course to improve my English proficiency before the programme begins. Here I will specify the courses that I would like to take and the qualifications I hope to obtain.

There are two courses for which I would like to registrate in your summer course. The first one is General English, Block 3, starting on August 17 and the second is Spoken English, Block 4, starting on September 7. At the end of both courses, I hope I can get the formal diplomas.

The study in your summer course will benefit my stay in Britain and my study in the University of Edinburgh. With the improvement of the Egnlish skills I can be free from those linguistic barriers.

Furthermore, when I return to my homeland, the qualifications will benefit me as well as my department. The department is going to set two advanced courses for senior students. They must be instructed in English in order to improve *students English skills*. So with the qualifications I obtain here, I will be the most competent person for that position.

All above are my motivation and purpose to take your summer English courses.

students English skills: the English skills of the students

Sample Writing 2: (Score: 7)

I want to take two summer courses from 27 July to 4 September in Edinburgh University.

The courses are Advanced Text Analysis and Translation and English for Literary Studies. I have advanced knowledge of German. This is required by the first course mentioned above, and I am going to teach English literature. I hope I can get a certificate from these courses.

In our country, *there are short of teachers who teach English literature*. I hope I could fill in this gap when I return with the qualifications. In addition, we should do further research in English literature, which is one of the most outstanding and influential literatures in the world, and promote our academic level in this area. In this way we can borrow excellent aspects from English literature and in turn raise our literature level.

there are short of teachers who teach English literature: teachers of English literature are badly needed

Sample Writing 3: (Score: 6)

I have read the general introduction of summer courses. And according to my speciality and interest, the courses I am going to take are as follows: General English, Spoken English and English Literary Studies.

Because I want to attain MSc in applied linguistics, General English is very useful for listening, speaking, reading and writing; and Spoken English and Literary Studies will enhance my knowledge of English literature. In addition, I am going to *continue to* be engaged in English language teaching after I *come to* our country. Therefore, I think these courses are very important for me.

continue to: This phrase should be omitted here.
come to: come back to

Appendices (附录)

1. A Brief Introduction to the IELTS Test
(IELTS 考试简介)

　　为了检验要去英国学习的非英语国家学生的英语能力，以英国文化委员会为主的若干英国机构近三十年来先后设计过数个考试。这些考试由于受新的语言学理论、语言教学理论和语言测试理论的影响，大多在使用一段时间后就显得过时，继而被新的考试所取代。目前在使用的最重要的此种考试是 International English Language Testing System（IELTS），俗称"英国使馆考试"，亦被称作"雅词"考试。

　　IELTS 是以要在英语环境中学习或培训的母语为其他语言的人为测试对象的英语考试，它的前身是 ELTS 考试（English Language Testing Service）。ELTS 由英国剑桥大学当地考试辛迪加设计，由英国文化委员会在海外组织，对象是要去英国高等学校学习或参加技术培训的非英语国家公民。因此，考试侧重于检验考生以英语为工具从事专业学习的能力。后来澳大利亚高校国际开发署参与考试工作，因而易名为 IELTS。首份 IELTS 试卷于 1990 年 4 月开始在中国使用。

　　IELTS 考试分听、读、写、说四个部分，每部分的满分为 9 分，总分是四部分成绩的平均。听力、阅读和总分可以有 0.5 分，如 5.5，6.5 等，写作和口试只有整数分。计算总分的方法是四个部分的成绩相加除以 4，如遇小数则或舍或入（0.5 除外）。小数为 0.25、0.375、0.75 和 0.875 时向上进一个分数段。例如：（6+6+6+7）÷4=6.25，总成绩为 6.5 分；（5.5+6+6+7）÷4=6.125，总成绩为 6 分。

　　目前我国公派到英国学习的访问学者和攻读硕士、博士学位的研究生均需参加此考试。一般来说，访问学者要 6 分、研究生要 6.5 分方可赴英，个别学校和专业则要求 7 分。越来越多的澳大利亚学校在录取海外学生时要求申请人参加 IELTS 考试并获得 6 至 7 分的成绩。因此 IELTS 考试在我国正逐渐成为一个重要的出国考试。

　　IELTS 考试的听力、阅读和写作部分在上午举行，口试在下午。上午的顺序是：听力（约 30 分钟），阅读（60 分钟），写作（60 分钟）。零散考生在英国驻华使馆文化教育处参加考试，国家公派的一些奖学金项目候选人在三个培训点（北京语言文化大学出国人员培训部、上海外国语大学出国人员培训部、成都科技大学出国人员培训部）之一参加培训后，由英国使馆文化教育处官员携考题赴这些培训点考试。

　　与 TOEFL、EPT 等考试相比，IELTS 考试的最大特点是对考生的英语交际能力进行测试，重点放在以英语为工具解决专业学习中的听、读、写、说实际问题方面，从而较好地避免了考生"高分低能"的现象。很多英语考试的听力、阅读，甚至写作试题均采用多项选择形式，这无疑增加了考生猜测的机会。并且由于词汇、语法题占一定比例，考生可通过在短期内大量地背单词和做语法题在考试中获得较高的"知识分"。由于有"知识"和猜测因素的作用,考生的成绩不能客观地反映其使用英语的实际能力。IELTS 考试在这方面有很大不同。

与其他主要英语考试相比,IELTS 考试的听力部分的特点亦是多项选择题数量很少,且以在数个图(而不是在数行文字)中选择为主。比如在一段听力对话中,A 告诉 B 要在某个银行门口约会,并描述赴约的路线。四个选择分别是四个街区平面图,在每个图中银行所处的位置不同,要求考生根据录音内容指出哪一幅图是对话中所描述的图。大部分题不是多项选择题,要由考生根据录音内容填空。比如,考生要答出录音中描述的某个事件发生的时间、地点。再比如,考生要根据录音内容简要回答 which, what, why, who 等问题。很多考生的一个共同困难是,不仅要边听边读,还要边写。如果没有做过大量的针对性很强的练习,又不熟悉这种听力考试的形式,要想获得理想的分数是比较困难的。这一部分共有 40 道题左右。

IELTS 考试的阅读部分由三至四篇文章构成,有 40 个左右的问题。它的最大特点是大部分题不是传统的多项选择题。比如,试题中的一篇文章有 8 段,问题中列出 12 个小标题,要求考生根据每段的内容从 12 个小标题中挑出本段的小标题。再比如,文章描述某一过程(如打捞沉船),要求考生把问题中列出的若干个步骤按其在过程中的先后顺序排序。试题还可能要求考生从列出的十几个单词、词组中选择正确答案填入一篇短文,其中一部分词或词组为干扰性选择,答题时有时还需参考试题中的另一篇文章。由于干扰因素很多,猜对的可能性几乎为零。IELTS 考试阅读部分与其他阅读考试的另一重大区别是,IELTS 考试不仅不含语法和词汇题,反而可能会列出若干关键词和定义,以帮助考生更好地理解。

写作分两部分:Task 1 和 Task 2 。Task 1 一般要求考生写一篇不少于 150 个词的短文描述所给的一个图(流程图、剖面图、曲线图等)或表,或根据一篇短文的内容写一份报告。比如,描述某一国家若干年内人口增减情况。再比如,描述一个欧洲城市分别在 1950、1970 和 1990 年中各种交通车辆的运营情况。试卷建议考生在 20 分钟内完成本部分。Task 2 一般要求考生就某问题提出解决的方法;为某一观点辩护;比较或对比一些根据和意见;评价或反驳一些论点;提供一般真实的报告。比如,"科学技术的发展将使传统文化丧失,这是不可避免的。科学技术与传统文化是不能共存的。在多大程度上你同意或不同意这个观点? 为你的回答提供论据。"再比如,你向英国一所大学申请留学生奖学金。申请书的最后部分要求你报告自己所从事的专业情况和将来的一些打算。试卷建议考生在 40 分钟内完成本部分。

IELTS 考试的口试部分约 15 分钟。考官会把整个考试分为四个阶段。1. 一般性对话:考官提问,考生回答。内容主要是个人情况,如家庭、工作、教育等。2. 某一话题的引申:在前一段对话的基础上,考官自然地接过一个话题,让考生较详细地描述某一事物或发表对某事的看法。比如让考生比较家乡和另一城市的区别;让考生谈对城市交通现状和未来的看法。3. 使用提示卡(cue card):考生从桌上抽取一张卡片,根据上面所写的某个假定的情况进行询问。比如考生要根据提示卡假设自己是一个新到英国的外国学生,在学校的住房办公室询问有关租房的情况。这一部分主要由考生提问,考官回答。4. 将来的打算:谈话内容从假设的语言环境中回到自然对话,考官让考生谈 IELTS 考试之后的打算,话题主要围绕何时出国、选择了哪所学校、进修计划等内容。口试不仅考学生回答、描述等方面的能力,还考学生能否用得体的语气、词汇等来询问、请求等。换言之,口试非常注重考生的语言交际能力。

IELTS 考试的写作和口试部分的评分要参考很详细的评分标准，但在一定程度上受考官主观看法的影响。阅读和听力部分是客观题，有标准答案，一般来说有百分之六十五的正确率可得 6 分。

与其他几种英语考试相比，IELTS 考试的另一特点是试卷重复使用。该考试的听、读、写部分不断有新的试题出笼，同时也有旧的试题被淘汰。目前有四五套试题（version）在使用，每次考试用不同的组合方式以尽量避免大规模重复。即使如此，仍有考生因第一次考试未达到所要求的分数段而再次参加考试时遇到做过的 version 。考试部门要求考生两次考试的间隔不少于三个月。

目前 IELTS 考试的费用为 70 英镑，报考时按外汇牌价收取人民币。如欲询问有关考试事宜，应与英国驻华使馆文化教育处联系，地址是：

北京
东三环北路 8 号
亮马河办公楼四层
英国大使馆文化教育处
邮编：100026

2. Criterion of the Writing Test
（写作测试评分标准）

Score 9

The reader finds the essay completely satisfactory. A point of view is presented and developed, either arguing for and supporting one position or considering alternative positions by presenting and discussing relevant ideas and evidence. The argument proceeds logically through the text with a clear progression of ideas. There is plentiful material. A wide range of vocabulary is used appropriately. The reader sees no errors in word formation or spelling. A wide range of sentence structures is used accurately and appropriately.

Score 8

This answer does not fully achieve level 9 in communicative quality, arguments, ideas and evidence. There is a good range of appropriate vocabulary. The reader sees no significant errors in word formation or spelling. The range of sentence structures used is good, and is well controlled for accuracy and appropriateness.

Score 7

The reader finds this a satisfactory essay which generally communicates fluently and only rarely causes strain. A point of view is presented, although it may be unclear at times whether a single position is being taken or alternative positions being considered. The argument has a clear progression overall although there may be minor isolated problems. Ideas and evidence are relevant and sufficient but more specific detail may seem desirable. The range of vocabulary is fairly good and vocabulary is usually used appropriately. Errors in word formation are rare and, while spelling errors do occur, they are not intrusive. A satisfactory range of sentence structures occurs and there are only occasional, minor flaws in the control of sentence structure.

Score 6

The reader finds this a mainly satisfactory essay which communicates with some degree of fluency. Although there is sometimes strain for the reader, control of organisational patterns and devices is evident. A point of view is presented although it may be unclear whether a single position is being taken or alternative positions are being considered. The progression of the argument is not always clear, and it may be difficult to distinguish main ideas from supporting material. The relevance of some ideas or evidence may be dubious and some specific support may seem desirable. The range of vocabulary sometimes appears limited accompanied by the inappropriateness of its use. Minor limitations of, or errors in, word choice sometimes intrude on the reader. Word formation and spelling errors occur but are only slightly intrusive. Sentence structures are generally adequate but the reader may feel that control is achieved by the use of a restricted range of structures or, in contrast, that the use of a wide variety of structures is not marked by the same level of structural accuracy.

Score 5

This is an essay which often causes strain for the reader. While the reader is aware of an overall lack of fluency, there is a sense of an answer which has underlying coherence. The essay introduces ideas although there may not be many of them or they may be insufficiently developed. Arguments are presented but may lack clarity, relevance, consistency or support. The range of vocabulary and appropriateness of its use are limited. Lexical confusion and incorrect word choice are noticeable. Word formation and spelling errors may be quite intrusive. There is a limited range of sentence structures and the greatest accuracy is achieved in short, simple sentences. Errors in such areas as agreement of tenses and of subjects and verbs are noticeable.

Score 4

This essay attempts communication but meaning comes through only after considerable effort by the reader. There are signs of a point of view but main ideas are difficult to distinguish from supporting materials and the amount of support is inadequate. Such evidence and ideas as are presented may not be relevant. There is no clear progression to the argument. The range of vocabulary is often inadequate and/or inappropriate. Word choice causes serious problems for the reader. Word formation and spelling errors cause severe strain for the reader. Limited control of sentence structures, even short and simple ones, is evident. Errors in such areas as agreement of tenses, and of subjects and verbs cause severe strain for the reader.

Score 3

The seriousness of the problems in this essay prevents meaning from coming through more than spasmodically. The essay has few ideas and no apparent development. Such evidence and ideas as are presented are irrelevant. There is little comprehensible point of view or argument. The reader is aware of gross inadequacies of vocabulary, word forms and spelling. Control of sentence structures is evident only occasionally and errors predominate.

Score 2

The writing displays no ability to communicate. There is evidence of one or two ideas without development. The reader sees no control of word choice, word forms and spelling. There is little or no evidence of control of sentence structures.

Score 1

The writing appears to be by a virtual non-writer, containing no assessable strings of English writing. If an answer is wholly or almost wholly copied from the source materials it is scored in this category.

Score 0

Should only be used where a candidate did not attend or did not attempt this question in any way.